Bookwebs

Bookwebs

A Brainstorm of Ideas
for the Primary Classroom

Barbara LeCroy
University of Southern Mississippi

Bonnie Holder
University of Southern Mississippi

1994
TEACHER IDEAS PRESS
A Division of
Libraries Unlimited, Inc.
Englewood, Colorado

This book is dedicated to our husbands,
Clarence and Glenn.

TEACHER IDEAS PRESS
A Division of Libraries Unlimited, Inc.
P.O. Box 6633
Englewood, CO 80155-6633
1-800-237-6124

Library of Congress Cataloging-in-Publication Data

LeCroy, Barbara B.
    Bookwebs : a brainstorm of ideas for the primary classroom /
Barbara LeCroy, Bonnie Holder.
    xi, 193 p. 22x28 cm.
    Includes bibliographical references and index.
    ISBN 1-56308-109-1
    1. Education, Primary--Activity programs.   I. Holder, Bonnie.
II. Title.
LB1537.L36   1994
372.24'1--dc20   93-44318
                                                              CIP

Acknowledgments

We wish to thank our many students, public school teachers, and university faculty and staff who have encouraged us along the way, and the student who illustrated the book for us, W. H. Goff.

Contents

Animal Stories

Fantasy

x ⅋ Contents

Themes

1

Introduction

ॐ

Children's books. Basals. Whole language. Integrating literature across the curriculum. Responding to literature. Which of these facilitates an early appreciation for books by young students, whets their imagination, develops critical thinking and other reading skills, allows educators to design exercises to meet the individual needs of students, empowers teachers, and puts joy back into the profession of teaching?

The whole-language impact has revealed the need to integrate subjects across the curriculum. Yet, many teaching professionals view children's literature and the teaching of reading and other curricular areas as separate entities that must be handled individually; others may want to establish a whole-language classroom but do not know how to go about the task. Children's literature can facilitate the transformation.

Why Children's Books?

In addition to developing a positive attitude toward reading, children's books provide valuable experiences for primary school students by connecting them with our national heritage, introducing them to other cultural groups, and giving them insight into the problems and promises of the contemporary world. Literature exposes students to rich, colorful language through prose and poetry and expands vocabulary in meaningful contexts while providing effective language models.

Until recently, the inclusion of children's literature in basal reading programs usually was limited to the abbreviated stories in the readers and to teachers' manual suggestions for using literature as enrichment or extension activities. A more extensive use of the children's literature offered in basal readers can enhance the basic material and amplify the potential of learning opportunities. Stories presented in the basal can be supplemented with selections from children's literature, or, for more cohesive experiences, more interesting or appropriate literature can be selected to replace a basal selection.

Integrating Literature in the Whole-Language Classroom

Many school districts in the United States and Canada are relinquishing basal readers in favor of instructional materials that promote learning in the meaningful format of whole-language classrooms. The widespread acceptance of the whole-language philosophy derives from its inclusion of children's books. The cooperative, integrated whole-language classroom is enhanced by books that develop an appreciation of literature and also, by design, develop reading skills. Vocabulary, spelling, imagination, and critical thinking are developed as reading and writing are used in tandem in the classroom. In addition to linking reading and writing, children's literature can be used across all subject areas of the primary grades to give added depth to the subject matter presented.

Empowerment and Joy

Teachers can experience the joy of learning with students as books are cooperatively selected, shared, and discussed. As students become more enthusiastic about reading, opportunities will emerge for activities once stifled by the format of the basal program. As teachers begin to put aside the basals and saturate the classroom with literature, they will need resources and guidebooks to help them select, plan, and coordinate successful book/activity programs. This book is such a guide.

Purpose of This Book

Bookwebs is designed to help primary grade teachers identify usable alternatives to the basal reader in the traditional classroom. In *Bookwebs*, teachers will find a variety of whole-language activities that can be used as starting points for integrating literature across the curriculum. The activities can be used to extend literary experiences across the primary grades curriculum and to foster the students' social, emotional, and cognitive development. The interrelated, subject-specific activity suggestions presented in each chapter ensure that the teaching of skills will not occur in isolation or through skill sheets but in real-life activity in a classroom setting. Child-centered activities and bulletin boards are used to promote reading and writing in an environment that emphasizes literacy and literary appreciation.

The Books in *Bookwebs*

Bookwebs features many selections representing the broad spectrum of children's literature. Books were selected by taking the core book or theme and brainstorming to come up with a list of related concepts or ideas; these concepts and ideas were used in selecting related books. The books are appropriate for most students between the ages of five and eight. An attempt was made to concentrate on current publications while retaining selected classics.

Structure of the Book

Fifteen books are featured as "core books," around which can be spun an entire web of interrelated language arts, math, science, social studies, and creative arts activities. Each of these core books is the focus of one chapter; the chapters are grouped into sections based on the type of book featured: picture story books, folklore, animal stories, and fantasy. In the final section of the book, three chapters are based on themes (family, friendship, and holidays) rather than specific books.

Bookweb Schematic

Each chapter is introduced with a bookweb, or schematic representation of the books used in each curricular area. At the center of each bookweb is the core book or theme; arrayed about it are the subject areas with a list of the books used for the activities in that subject area. The bookweb shows the relationship of the books to each other and to the content areas in which they are used. At a glance, teachers can see which books are needed for particular subject area activities and which books are used in more than one subject area. (See page 4.)

Information on Core Book or Theme

The first section of each chapter offers a bibliographic citation to the core book, a plot summary, and brief sections detailing the book's genre and the subject areas in which the book may be used. The teacher can use this information to judge the appropriateness of the book for a particular group of students.

Brainstorming Starters

Following the preliminary information about the book, a list of related words is offered. These may help the teacher direct students' brainstorming or fill in gaps after the brainstorming session.

Suggested Activities

The bulk of each chapter comprises suggested activities that incorporate literature in all subject areas. In most chapters, two or more activities are offered for each of the following subject areas: language arts, math, science, social studies, and creative arts. Each activity can be used alone or in conjunction with other activities. Most of the activities can be completed in one or two class periods, although a few (for example, growing seeds or hatching eggs) extend over several weeks. Many of the activities are done in small groups or pairs. No exotic materials are needed. Common art supplies, such as construction paper, buttons, paper plates, and glue, are required for many of the activities; a few require costumes or items that children bring from home (for example, stuffed animals, measuring utensils, or musical instruments.

An effort has been made to include a broad array of activities, from journal writing to field trips. The activities that focus on reading, thinking, writing, and doing can be used to develop new skills or to review or reinforce those skills. The activities are child-centered, promote collaborative learning, and avoid the use of skill sheets. Many of the activities (for example, gardening) are designed for use in more than one content area.

This portion of each chapter concludes with ideas for child-centered, activity-related bulletin boards. Some of these bulletin boards serve as display panels for projects made during the activities; others are activities in themselves. In either case, students can help to design and create the bulletin boards.

Annotated Bibliography

Each chapter concludes with an annotated list of the books used in the chapter, as well as some other related books that are not referenced in the chapter.

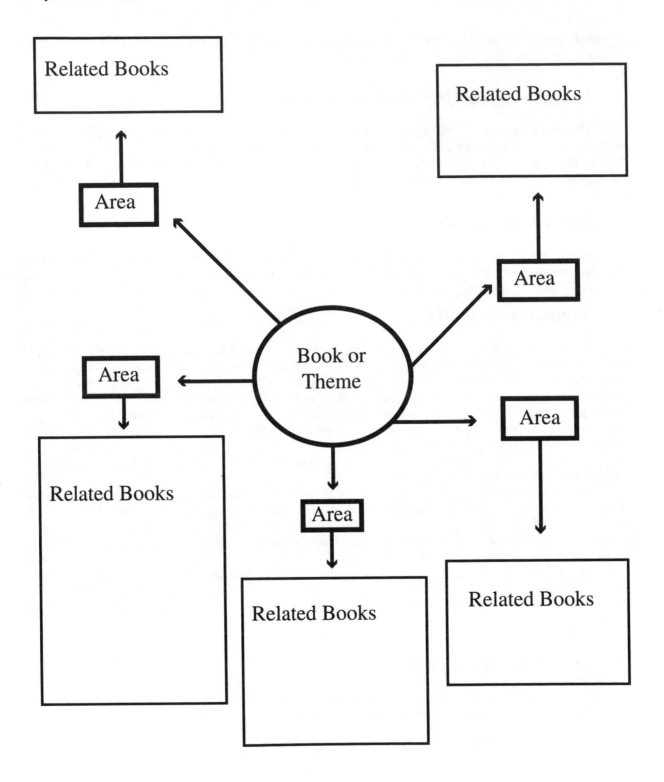

How to Use This Book

This book is not meant to be used in front-to-back fashion. Teachers should browse through the book, selecting a chapter that features a core book suited to their class. After browsing through the chapter, the teacher may select one or more activities to tie in with the book. In most cases, a number of alternatives are offered. For example, science activities may relate to wind or the formation of bubbles; again, the teacher would pick the activity best suited to the class.

After deciding to use a particular selection, the teacher can spark the students' interest through prereading promotion: looking at the book and its jacket and illustrations, discussing the author and illustrator, or determining whether the book received any honors. The teacher may use leading questions, directed dialogue, pictures and other visuals, or related books to introduce the students to the theme of the selection. Finally, the teacher discusses the theme of the story and reads the story aloud to the class.

After the book is read, the teacher may ask the class to brainstorm related words or concepts. The students' ideas should be listed on the chalkboard. The teacher may start the brainstorming session with a word or two from the Brainstorming Starters and then use the list to fill in gaps in the final list. This list of ideas can be used as students verify previous knowledge about the information generated, establish a purpose for reading, and extend the ideas established. Following or during the brainstorming session, the teacher may read the book again.

Most activities start with the reading of one or more books. The teacher should keep the core books and the related books on display until all related activities are completed. It is important to remember that the suggested activities are just that. A teacher may select only those activities that are suitable for the class or may modify the suggested activities to suit the students.

Most of the activities direct students to make some kind of a product (a big book, costume, report or chart, mural, and so forth), and teachers are instructed to allow students to display or share these products. Sufficient time to share them should be allowed.

Summary

The purposes of whole-language learning can be reduced to two. First, to ensure that skills are not learned in isolation but in a sensible context and second, to foster an interest in (or, better, a love of) reading. As teachers begin to direct literature-based learning, the whole-language classroom becomes a community of learners, with the teacher and students reflecting and reinforcing their interest and enthusiasm.

Picture Story Books

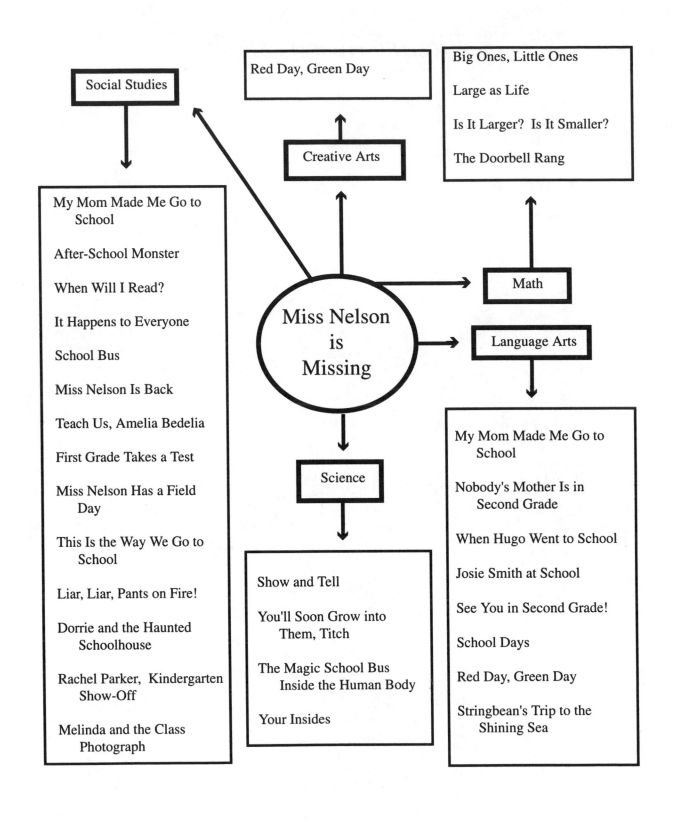

Social Studies

My Mom Made Me Go to School

After-School Monster

When Will I Read?

It Happens to Everyone

School Bus

Miss Nelson Is Back

Teach Us, Amelia Bedelia

First Grade Takes a Test

Miss Nelson Has a Field Day

This Is the Way We Go to School

Liar, Liar, Pants on Fire!

Dorrie and the Haunted Schoolhouse

Rachel Parker, Kindergarten Show-Off

Melinda and the Class Photograph

Red Day, Green Day

Creative Arts

Big Ones, Little Ones

Large as Life

Is It Larger? Is It Smaller?

The Doorbell Rang

Miss Nelson is Missing

Math

Language Arts

My Mom Made Me Go to School

Nobody's Mother Is in Second Grade

When Hugo Went to School

Josie Smith at School

See You in Second Grade!

School Days

Red Day, Green Day

Stringbean's Trip to the Shining Sea

Science

Show and Tell

You'll Soon Grow into Them, Titch

The Magic School Bus Inside the Human Body

Your Insides

2

Miss Nelson Is Missing

ঽ

Allard, Harry. *Miss Nelson Is Missing*. Illustrated by James Marshall. Boston: Houghton Mifflin, 1977.

Genre: Picture Book

Summary: The students in room 207 learn to appreciate their teacher after Viola Swamp serves as a substitute for Miss Nelson.

Content Areas: Language arts, math, science, social studies, and creative arts. This book can be used to introduce a language arts or social studies unit on the beginning or ending of the school year.

Brainstorming Starters:

School	Misbehave
Teacher	Act up
Substitute teacher	Missed
Principal	Detective
Lessons	Terrible
Story hour	Secret
Books	Witch
Homework	

Activities for Language Arts

"Hello, I Am"

At the beginning of a new school year read *Miss Nelson Is Missing* and *My Mom Made Me Go to School* to the class. Ask students to discuss how they felt about beginning school or a new school year. After the students share their feelings about starting school, divide them into groups of two. Have each student divide a sheet of paper into four sections. Instruct the students to write something about themselves in each section. Suggest section headings such as favorite foods, ice cream, colors, sports or games, or pets. Have the students in each pair exchange sheets and use the information to introduce each other to the class. Encourage the students to say nice things about their partners. Take a picture of each student as he or she is introduced. Provide art supplies for mounting the pictures and have students write four to six descriptive words below their pictures. Place the pictures on the bulletin board under a heading selected by the class.

"Visiting Other Classes"

Read *Nobody's Mother Is in Second Grade* and ask students how they would disguise their mother if she wanted to enroll in the class. List the ideas on the chalkboard and have students select the best disguises. Ask the students which grade they would like to be in if they could be in another grade. Encourage them to give reasons for their answers. Ask if they would go in disguise to the other class.

If possible, arrange a class visit to a middle school, junior high, or high school. Tell the students they will have the opportunity to observe classrooms and activities to find out what it would be like if they changed grades. Divide the class into groups and have each group state what it wants to learn about the grades to be visited. Write the questions on charts so that groups can compare their inquiries. Have each group prepare questions for its members to investigate during the visit. After returning from the visit, have the groups make charts to report what they learned. Have students share their findings and discuss whether there were any surprises. If a visit is not possible, ask students to interview older siblings or friends and report the findings to the class.

"School Days"

This activity can be used at the beginning of the school year as plans are being made for learning activities, or it can be adapted for an end-of-year activity as students prepare for summer vacation. Read and discuss the events in *When Hugo Went to School*, *Josie Smith at School*, and *See You in Second Grade!* If this activity is used at the beginning of the school year, have individual students or groups of students share what they want to learn during the school year. If this activity is to be used at the end of a school year, have them recall interesting things that have occurred during the school year. Divide the class into groups and have each group write a story about one of the events. These stories can be illustrated and shared with the class. Or, have individual students write stories about something that happened during the school year and share these stories in small groups.

"Show and Tell"

Read *School Days* and *Red Day, Green Day* to the class. Ask students to name the things that happen on a typical day in your classroom. Plan a special show-and-tell day to let others know what happens on a typical day in the classroom. Help students design and make invitations for adult friends, parents, or grandparents. In the invitations, ask guests to be prepared to describe a typical day when they were in school. Divide the class into groups to brainstorm how to show and tell the class about something they learned during the school year. On the special day, have each group show and tell what they have been learning; then ask the visitors to share their experiences with the class. Allow the students to ask the visitors questions about when they were in school. After the visit, divide the class into pairs to project what they will someday tell their children about when they were in school. Have each pair share its ideas with the class.

"Summer Vacation"

Near the end of the school year, share *See You in Second Grade!* and *Stringbean's Trip to the Shining Sea* with the class. After discussing these books, have the class brainstorm what they have planned or might do during summer vacation. Have students tell which ideas include activities that involve learning. Divide the class into groups to plan a vacation trip. Provide each group with several pieces of paper that have been cut to the size of postcards. Instruct each group to illustrate the postcards based on the itinerary of its planned trip. Have each group write a message about the places they illustrated. Have a group of students make a mailbox out of a cardboard box, and have each group place its postcards in the box. Appoint several students to deliver the postcards. Have the students exchange the postcards. The postcards can be placed on a bulletin board about vacations.

Activities for Math

"As Tall As"

Introduce the concepts tall, taller, and tallest by asking students to name things that are tall and recording the responses on the chalkboard. Show pictures of animals, such as a giraffe, a monkey, and a mouse, and ask students to compare the sizes. Read *Big Ones, Little Ones* and *Large as Life* and discuss the sizes of the animals and the ladybug in the stories. Review with students the objects listed as tall and add objects that are short.

Ask the class to list two objects in the classroom that are tall, such as a window, set of shelves, or a door. Have students share their lists. Identify one item common to most of the lists. Measure the students to see how many are as tall as the item identified. Make two charts on the board, one showing how many are taller, as tall as, or shorter than the item, and the other listing names under tall, taller, and tallest. Have students draw a picture of something shorter than they are and use the story starter "I am taller than . . . " to write about the picture. Display the finished pictures in the classroom. Later in the year, measure the class again.

"Estimating Measurements"

Show the class the pictures in *Is It Larger? Is It Smaller?* and discuss how the book explains size. Write the words *large*, *small*, *long*, *short*, *larger*, *shorter*, *longer*, *smaller*, *largest*, *longest*, *shortest*, and *smallest* on the chalkboard. Have students discuss and demonstrate the words. Ask what tools we use to measure items for size. Show students a six-inch ruler with each inch shown in a different color. Suggest that rough measurements can be made by estimating and comparing without rulers. Have students form pairs; have each pair compare two pencils and then three pencils. Have volunteers to hold up the longest pencil, the smallest pencil, and so forth. Have two volunteers compare the sizes of their shoes, hands, and arms and use one of the words on the chalkboard to describe their sizes. Ask how you could measure the circumference of a wrist or head. Divide students into groups to measure wrists and heads using string you provide for that purpose. Ask the students to use the words on the chalkboard to compare the sizes of their wrists and heads. Have each group make a list of things in the room that can be compared, such as books, pieces of chalk, and crayons. Then have the groups trace the outlines of these items on a sheet of paper to show their relative sizes. Display the pictures in the math area.

"Sharing"

Read *The Doorbell Rang* to the class and let students discuss things that they have had to share with family or friends. Introduce division by dividing the class into pairs and giving each pair two paper plates and twelve colored-paper cookies. Have each pair divide the cookies so that each person has the same number. After this, divide the class into groups of three; give each group twelve cookies made from a different color of paper. Have the groups divide these cookies so that each person has the same number of cookies. Have the students look at the cookies they got the first time and tell whether they got fewer cookies the second time. Following this discussion, divide the class into groups of four; give each group twelve cookies in another color. Ask them to divide these so that each person has an equal number of cookies; have the students compare this number of cookies to the earlier groups of cookies. When the students are able to tell what happens to their share of the cookies when more people are added to the groups, give each group twelve real cookies to share while drawing a picture of twelve cookies being divided by four students. Display the pictures in the classroom.

Activities for Science

"Detective Bubbles"

Discuss *Show and Tell* and *Miss Nelson Is Missing*. Discuss what happened with the bubbles in *Show and Tell* and what a detective is in *Miss Nelson Is Missing*. Following this discussion, have each student write a description of another student in the class. The description should include eye color, clothing, and other features. Have students read their descriptions and let the class guess who is being described.

Tell the class they are going to become science detectives to find out information about bubbles. Ask students to name things that are shaped like bubbles, from balloons to domes on buildings. Divide the class into groups and give each group a list of things to find out about the bubbles through research. Have students locate descriptions of bubbles in science trade books, magazines, encyclopedias, or science books. Guide their research through questions listed on a sheet, such as "Are they solid or liquid?" "Can they change?" "How are bubbles formed?" "What happens to them?" "What makes them stick together?" and "What makes them pop?" Explain what a "Most Wanted" (criminal information) poster is and show an example. Have each group write what it learned about bubbles in

MOST WANTED

BUBBLES

1. Bubbles have thin, watery skin.

2. The color of bubbles can be changed by adding food coloring.

3. When blown with warm air, bubbles rise.

4. Even if a bubble is first square, the shape will become round.

5. Glycerin may help give bubbles longer life.

6. A bubbles' number one enemy is dryness.

7. Bubbles pop when touched with a dry object.

8. Bubbles range in size from smaller than a dime to larger than a basketball.

the form of descriptions on "Most Wanted" sheets. Have each group share its findings with the class. Ask each group to make a list of common household items, such as funnels or plastic rings, that could be used for blowing bubbles. After compiling the lists, ask students to bring one such item to class for a bubble-blowing experiment.

"Bubble Blowing"

Plan a bubble-blowing experiment. Divide the class into groups. Give each group straws, spools, shallow pans, and other devices for blowing. (These other devices include the household items identified in the previous exercise.) Make a bubble mixture with glycerin, liquid detergent, and water. After blowing a few bubbles, add more glycerin and show students how this allows them to blow larger bubbles. Ask students to see what happens when they touch bubbles with wet and dry objects. Use drinking straws to measure bubbles by deciding whether each bubble is smaller than a drinking straw. Use a wet stick or ruler to measure the largest bubble. Have students use string wet with bubble solution to measure the circumference of bubbles. After the experiment, have students list what they learned. Have them share their findings with their group and then with the class.

"Life Cycle—Growing and Changing"

Show pictures of baby and adult animals. Have volunteers match the pictures. Ask if all things grow and change. Have students cut out pictures of babies and older children and place them on poster board for a display. Ask students to tell what they looked like as babies and how they have changed. Read and discuss how Titch handled the problem of growth in *You'll Soon Grow into Them, Titch*. After discussing problems related to changes, ask students what they think they will be like in two years and in five years. Following this discussion, ask if all things grow at the same rate. Have them give examples, such as hair, arms, and legs. Read *The Magic School Bus Inside the Human Body* and *Your Insides*. Have students identify and name body parts we see, such as arms and eyes. Ask them to brainstorm parts inside our bodies, such as heart and lungs. If possible, have a school nurse visit and discuss muscles, brain, stomach, and other internal parts. Ask her to allow students to use the stethoscope to listen to their hearts. Have students list the work of muscles, the brain, and the stomach. Divide the class into small groups and have them make a large outline of a student's body. (This can be done by having one student lie on butcher paper on the floor while other students draw an outline of his or her body.) Have the group draw lungs, heart, brain, muscles, and bones on the outline. The finished products can be displayed in the science area.

Activities for Social Studies

"Sometimes School Makes Me . . ."

To introduce this activity, ask how many students like school and how many dislike school. After counting the number for each response, ask how school makes them feel. Discuss the feelings identified. Ask students to identify the feelings of the characters as you read *My Mom Made Me Go to School*, *After-School Monster*, *When Will I Read?*, and *It Happens to Everyone*. Have students identify the characters, the events, and the solutions to the problems in the books. Then ask them to think about what they would have done if they had been the main character in each story. Divide the class into groups to think about being a new student in a school. Have two groups develop ideas on what a new student can do to make friends while two other groups decide what the groups or class can do to welcome a new member. Have each group present its ideas, and then have each group role-play a new-student situation to demonstrate their ideas.

"School Workers"

Display pictures of school buildings, schoolrooms, school offices, cafeterias, school buses, and pictures involving school workers. Ask the students to identify the workers who help make the school day go smoothly as you read *School Bus*; *Miss Nelson Is Back*; and *Teach Us, Amelia Bedelia*. For each book, have students name the person who was a school worker. Then ask students to identify the school workers pictured in the books. List the jobs or job titles on the chalkboard or a chart. Have the students brainstorm what each person does to help students. Have students generate questions to ask school workers about their jobs. Plan a walk around the school to identify the school's workers and allow students to ask them questions about their jobs. Divide into groups, with each group taking one school worker and telling how that person's job helps students learn or makes learning more comfortable. Ask each group to draw a picture of the worker and write a thank-you note below it. Place these in the hallway for workers and other students to read.

"School Activities"

Ask if all schools are alike. Have students who have attended different schools describe the other schools and compare them to the present school. Encourage students to think of all of the items or activities in the school that are for learning, such as pencils, desks, music lessons, or gym classes. As students name them, list them. Have students listen to *First Grade Takes a Test* and *Miss Nelson Has a Field Day*. Ask students which they would enjoy more: a test or a field day. Have them describe how learning is related to each. Give the groups the option of making a booklet about the school for new students or visitors or constructing a mural of various school activities.

Suggest that children in other countries may have similar feelings about school. Read *This Is the Way We Go to School*. Divide the class into research groups to find pictures of children in other countries going to school. Have the groups prepare to show the pictures to the class. If students cannot find pictures of schools in other countries, have them collect pictures of school objects and make a display.

"School Rules"

Ask the question "Why do you go to school?" Have students write a response in their journals. Allow students to read their responses aloud and then ask what kind of environment is best for learning. After students have responded to this question, have them think about things that students can do together to learn, for example, sharing books, keeping quiet during study time, or answering questions in class. Suggest that learning can be disrupted at school; have students name some of the interruptions that impede learning. Read *Liar, Liar, Pants on Fire!*; *Dorrie and the Haunted Schoolhouse*; *Rachel Parker, Kindergarten Show-Off*; and *Melinda and the Class Photograph*. Ask students to identify the disruptive or inappropriate actions in each book. Encourage students to think of things that make school more enjoyable and create a better atmosphere for learning. Divide into groups to compile a list of rules for classroom behavior. After each group has compiled its list, ask it to share with the class. After all of the groups have read their lists, make one chart of class rules. Display the chart.

Activities for Creative Arts

"Mural"

Provide art materials, such as magazines with pictures, a six-foot sheet of butcher paper, paints, crayons, markers, and glue, for students to use in making a mural. Have one group construct a picture about a classroom, another the cafeteria, the playground, and one the library. Students can cut out, draw, or make objects and place them on the mural.

"Color Days"

Read *Red Day, Green Day* to the class. Have students tell how the different colors were featured each day. Have the class decide if it would like to have different days such as the ones in the book. Suggest they might have polka-dot or checked days as well as color days. After deciding what each day will feature, send a note home to explain the activity to parents. Be sure to have extra materials available each day for students who might forget to bring the assigned color or pattern. Have students write in their journals each day about that day's activity.

"Colors in Bubbles"

Use this activity in conjunction with the science activities in "Detective Bubbles" and "Bubble Blowing." As students blow bubbles, have them identify the different colors they see in each bubble. Discuss reasons for the colors and provide a prism for students to identify colors. Have each student select one color and, using only that color, draw a picture that has bubbles in it. Display the pictures in the room.

Bulletin Boards

"Our Class"

Have the class select a caption for a bulletin board that will feature pictures of students. Write the caption on the board. Have each student place his or her picture and descriptive words (from the language arts activity "Hello, I Am") on the bulletin board.

"Summer Vacation"

Place a map of the United States in the center of the bulletin board with the phrase *Our Summer Vacation* written on the map. Have students select postcards they made in the language arts activity "Summer Vacation" and position the selected postcards on the map.

Related Books

Allard, Harry. *Miss Nelson Has a Field Day.* Illustrated by James Marshall. Boston: Houghton Mifflin, 1985.
Miss Swamp returns to Horace B. Smedley School to make a winner of the football team.

———. *Miss Nelson Is Back.* Illustrated by James Marshall. Boston: Houghton Mifflin, 1982.
Viola Swamp returns to room 207 when Miss Nelson becomes ill and the principal fails as a substitute.

———. *Miss Nelson Is Missing.* Illustrated by James Marshall. Boston: Houghton Mifflin, 1977.
The students in Room 207 learn to appreciate their teacher after Viola Swamp serves as a substitute for Miss Nelson.

Baer, Edith. *This Is the Way We Go to School.* Illustrated by Steve Bjorkman. New York: Scholastic, 1990.
Rhymes tell the story of how children around the world go to school.

Cohen, Miriam. *First Grade Takes a Test.* Illustrated by Lillian Hoban. New York: Greenwillow Books, 1980.
After a test, the teacher must persuade her students that tests do not measure everything.

———. *Liar, Liar, Pants On Fire!* Illustrated by Lillian Hoban. New York: Greenwillow Books, 1985.
Alex, a new boy in first grade, has difficulty making friends because he lies.

———. *See You in Second Grade!* Illustrated by Lillian Hoban. New York, Greenwillow Books, 1989.
The class recalls events of the year when the teacher takes them on an end-of-the-year picnic.

———. *When Will I Read?* Illustrated by Lillian Hoban. New York: Greenwillow Books, 1977.
Jim is anxious to learn to read in this story.

Cole, Joanna. *The Magic School Bus Inside the Human Body.* Illustrated by Bruce Degen. New York: Scholastic, 1989.
The class is swallowed by a boy and takes a tour of his body.

———. *Your Insides.* Illustrated by Paul Meisel. New York: Putnam, 1992.
This information book examines various parts of the body and how they work.

Coombs, Patricia. *Dorrie and the Haunted Schoolhouse.* New York: Clarion Books, 1992.
A little witch goes to witch school and causes an exciting adventure in this Dorrie story.

Crew, David. *School Bus.* Illustrated by the author. New York: Greenwillow Books, 1984.
This picture book shows a day's work of a school bus.

Delton, Judy. *My Mom Made Me Go to School.* Illustrated by Lisa McCue. New York: Doubleday 1991.
After many apprehensions about beginning school, Archie finds he likes kindergarten in this picture book.

Finzel, Julia. *Large as Life*. Illustrated by the author. New York: Lothrop, Lee & Shepard, 1991.
A ladybug compares large and small animals in this picture book.

Hennessy, B. G. *School Days*. Illustrated by Tracey Campbell. Pearson. New York: Viking Children's Books, 1990.
This story depicts a typical day in a multiethnic classroom of a primary school.

Hoban, Tana. *Big Ones, Little Ones*. New York: Greenwillow Books, 1976.
This book contains photographs of baby and adult animals.

———. *Is It Larger? Is It Smaller?* Photographs by the author. New York: Greenwillow Books, 1985.
Photographs are used to show size.

Hutchins, Pat. *The Doorbell Rang*. New York: Mulberry Books, 1986.
Each time the doorbell rings, two children must redivide their cookies in this counting book.

———. *You'll Soon Grow into Them, Titch*. New York: Greenwillow Books, 1983.
Titch adjusts to the problems of hand-me-down clothes that are too large.

Kunhardt, Edith. *Red Day, Green Day*. Illustrated by Marylin Hafner. New York: Greenwillow Books, 1992.
Show-and-tell in a kindergarten class features different colors every week.

Martin, Ann. *Rachel Parker, Kindergarten Show-Off*. Illustrated by Nancy Poydar. New York: Holiday House, 1992.
A humorous story about two kindergartners learning to be friends.

Moss, Marissa. *After-School Monster*. New York: Lothrop, Lee & Shepard, 1991.
When a little girl goes home to an empty house after school, she develops the courage to live with the monster of being alone.

Myers, Bernice. *It Happens to Everyone*. New York: Lothrop, Lee & Shepard, 1992.
Michael and his teacher experience many misfortunes on the first day of school.

Nabb, Magdalen. *Josie Smith at School*. Illustrated by Pirkko Vainio. New York: Macmillan, 1992.
Josie has many school adventures that did not turn out as she had planned.

Parish, Peggy. *Teach Us, Amelia Bedelia*. Illustrated by Lynn Sweat. New York: Greenwillow Books, 1977.
School is very different when Amelia Bedelia is the substitute teacher.

Pulver, Robin. *Nobody's Mother Is in Second Grade*. Illustrated by G. Brian Karas. New York: Penguin Books, 1992.
Cassandra comes up with a disguise for her mother to wear to school.

Rockwell, Anne. *When Hugo Went to School*. Illustrated by the author. New York: Macmillan, 1991.
When Hugo the dog goes to school, the principal will not let him in and he gets lost.

van der Beek, Deborah. *Melinda and the Class Photograph*. Minneapolis, Minn.: Carolrhoda Books, 1992.
Melinda does not want to have her picture taken at school.

Williams, Vera B. *Stringbean's Trip to the Shining Sea*. Illustrated by the author and Jennifer Williams. New York: Greenwillow Books, 1988.
A trip to the West Coast is told through picture postcards.

Woodruff, Elvira. *Show and Tell*. Illustrated by Denise Brunkus. New York: Holiday House, 1991.
The jar of bubbles Andy brings to show-and-tell takes the entire class on an unforgettable journey.

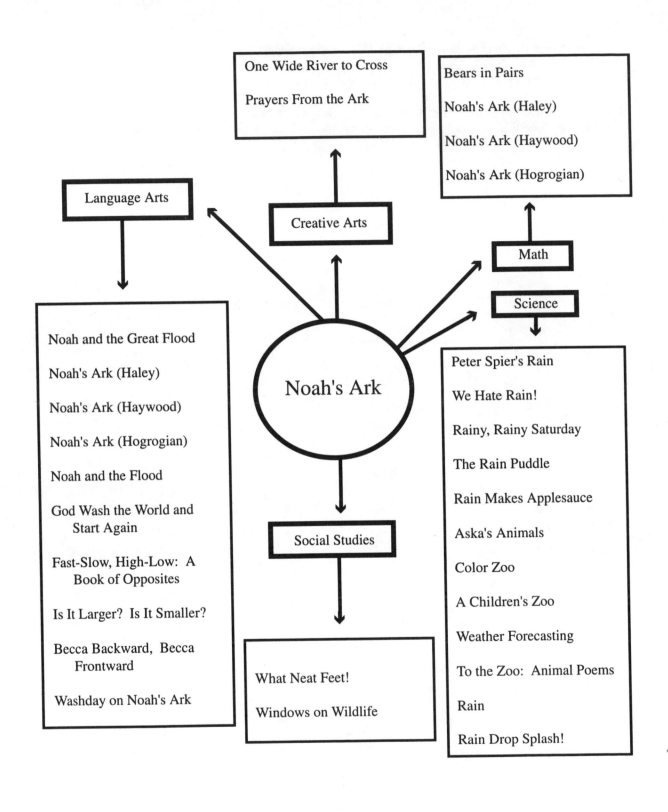

One Wide River to Cross

Prayers From the Ark

Bears in Pairs

Noah's Ark (Haley)

Noah's Ark (Haywood)

Noah's Ark (Hogrogian)

Language Arts

Creative Arts

Math

Science

Noah's Ark

Noah and the Great Flood

Noah's Ark (Haley)

Noah's Ark (Haywood)

Noah's Ark (Hogrogian)

Noah and the Flood

God Wash the World and
Start Again

Fast-Slow, High-Low: A
Book of Opposites

Is It Larger? Is It Smaller?

Becca Backward, Becca
Frontward

Washday on Noah's Ark

Social Studies

What Neat Feet!

Windows on Wildlife

Peter Spier's Rain

We Hate Rain!

Rainy, Rainy Saturday

The Rain Puddle

Rain Makes Applesauce

Aska's Animals

Color Zoo

A Children's Zoo

Weather Forecasting

To the Zoo: Animal Poems

Rain

Rain Drop Splash!

3

Noah's Ark

ॐ

Spier, Peter. *Noah's Ark*. Illustrated by the author. Garden City, N.Y.: Doubleday, 1977. (Caldecott Medal)

Genre: Picture story book

Summary: Detailed color illustrations of building the ark, the adventures aboard the ark, and beginning life after the flood.

Content Areas: Language arts, math, science, social studies, and creative arts. This book could be used to introduce a unit on opposites, pairs, rain, or animals.

Brainstorming Starters:

Rain	Day–Night
Rainbow	Sad–Happy
Ark	Dry–Wet
Pairs	Animals
Crowd	Messy
Slow	Dove
Inside–Outside	Olive branch

Activities for Language Arts

"Comparing Books"

Have available for display *Noah and the Great Flood* and several versions of the story of Noah's ark. Introduce each book by describing the differences in the illustrations. Give students three pieces of paper. Have them write *alike* on the first piece, *different* on the second, and *similar* on the third. Compare pictures in the books by holding up two books at a time and having students hold up the card that best compares them.

Discuss the concepts in the books *Fast-Slow, High-Low: A Book of Opposites*; *Is It Larger? Is It Smaller?*; and *Becca Backward, Becca Frontward*. Divide the class into several groups to identify pairs of opposite concepts in books about the ark. Introduce the following opposite concepts: inside–outside, sad–happy, slow–fast, big–little, tall–short, few–many, and high–low. Have each group find examples of these opposites in a selected book and show the examples to the class.

Introduce the concept of *crowded* by marking off a three-foot square with masking tape and then determining how many students can stand in the square before it becomes crowded. After deciding on the number, have students describe other crowded situations. Pictures of these situations can be drawn.

"Big Book"

After sharing *Fast-Slow, High-Low: A Book of Opposites* with the class, direct the students to rejoin the groups formed for the previous exercise. Give each group several large sheets of paper. Have the groups draw and label various opposite concepts. Make each student be responsible for drawing one opposite set, such as big–little. Create cover sheets that contain an illustration and a list of contributors. Complete the books by fastening the sheets together with three or four plastic rings. Shared finished books with the class and place them in the reading center.

"Story Starter"

After looking at books featuring Noah's ark, have students imagine that they were on the ark. The tall tale *Washday on Noah's Ark* (or the African folktale *God Wash the World and Start Again*) would enhance this activity. Have students write in response to the story starter, "If I had been Noah, I would have. . . ." A picture can be drawn to illustrate each story. When completed, stories and pictures can be shared with the class.

Activities for Math

"Feeding a Crowd"

After discussing the pictures in several versions of the story of Noah's ark, divide the class into groups. Ask each group to calculate how many hamburgers, fries, and glasses of milk would be needed to feed the class lunch for one, two, and three days. Have students prepare charts to show the calculations. Have each group display its chart. Compare the charts. Help the class compile the charts to project how much food would be needed for one day.

"Pairs of Animals"

After looking at one of the pictures in *Noah's Ark*, have each student jot down how many different animals are in that picture. Without looking again at the page, make a list on the chalkboard as students identify the animals pictured. Check to see if any animals were missed by showing the page again. Have pairs of students find pairs of animals in magazines. Have the students cut out the pictures and paste them on sheets of construction paper. When this has been completed, read *Bears in Pairs*. Have students count the number of pairs they found and have them count the animals two by two (i.e., two, four, six, etc.). Help those needing assistance in counting.

Activities for Science

"Weather Journal"

Share *Peter Spier's Rain*; *We Hate Rain!*; *Rainy, Rainy Saturday*; *The Rain Puddle*; *Rain Makes Applesauce*; and *Weather Forecasting* with the class. Brainstorm to find out what students know about where rain and water come from and whether the earth is mostly land or water. Have the class decide what it would like to know about rain and water. Allow students to answer their questions through research in science trade books, textbooks, and encyclopedias. Have students share their findings with the class.

Instruct students to keep weather entries in daily journals for the next month. Daily entries can be made by using words or pictures to describe the previous day's weather. After two weeks of recording weather, give students a calendar for the next two weeks. Have students predict the weather for the next two weeks by placing a symbol for sun, clouds, rain, snow, hot, cold, or wind on each day. Have students check their predictions daily. Prepare a chart to record the number of correct predictions each day. If possible, place a rain gauge on the school campus and assign a different student to check and record the amount of rain each day. At the end of the experiment, add up the amount of rain and how many days were sunny or rainy to determine which days the students' predictions were most accurate. Discuss what problems they encountered in predicting the weather.

"Flood"

After looking at books related to Noah and the flood, as well as *Rain*; *Rain Drop Splash!*; *We Hate Rain*; and *Peter Spier's Rain*, write the word *flood* on the chalkboard. Have students tell what they know about floods. Display pictures of flooded areas. Encourage students to inquire about floods in the area or floods that family and friends have experienced. Have students try to find out the causes and consequences of floods and report their findings to the class. If possible, have a person from the local civil defense office, a television or radio weather forecaster, or a representative of a local utility company talk with the class about what to do during floods or dangerous weather. Then have the class make a chart of safety rules. If it is not possible to have a resource person speak to the class, have students tell about a time when an event they had planned was rained out and what they did as a result.

"Food for Animals"

After looking at *Aska's Animals*; *Color Zoo*; and *A Children's Zoo*, list the animals found in the books. Divide the class into collaborative groups and assign each group five animals. Have each group research the eating habits of the assigned animals. Have each group report its findings. Compile a class collaborative report by drawing pictures of the animals eating. Place the report in the science center.

"Where Do Animals Live?"

Read aloud poems from *To the Zoo: Animal Poems*. Place one of the lists of animals made for the math activity "Pairs of Animals" or the science activity "Food for Animals" on the chalkboard. Divide the class into small groups to identify the habitats of animals. Give each group a poster board on which to write these five headings: Pond/Ocean, Desert, Sky, Forest/Woodlands, and North or South Pole. Assist students or allow them to use reference books as they write in or draw animals on the poster board under the proper headings. Compare the results of each group and clear up any misunderstandings.

A field trip to a museum or a zoo can be planned. Check with the zoo to see what animals are in it. Have students select an animal to study on the trip. Plan the things they are to observe, such as unusual animals, the ages of the animals, and the natural homes of animals in the zoo. Discuss how the zoo habitat is different from the animals' natural homes. (The habitats of animals can be observed in a museum with a natural history exhibit.) When you return to the classroom, have each student draw a picture of the animal he or she studied and write a paragraph about it.

Activities for Social Studies

"Animal Worth"

The value or worth of human and animal life can be emphasized by looking at different versions of the story of Noah's ark and *What Neat Feet!* Identify some of the animals on the ark and have students work in small groups to talk about and list the value of the animals identified. Encourage them to discuss the contribution of each animal to humans and to other animals. Have groups report to the class the value of each animal. After completing this assignment, have each group decide which animals it would take on the ark and why. Have each group report its decisions to the class and have the class discuss the consequences of the choices.

"Cleanliness"

Show pages at the beginning and end of *Noah's Ark* and discuss why the degree of cleanliness changed from the beginning to the end of the book. Discuss the need for taking care of animal pets and why cleanliness is important. Read *Windows on Wildlife* to show students how animals are cared for in zoos, wildlife parks, and aquariums. Appoint a clean-up team to take care of any classroom pets or to clean up the work areas of the classroom. The team should rotate daily and complete a checklist to show that the task was done.

Activities for Creative Arts

"Olive Branch"

Discuss the significance of the olive branch in *Noah's Ark*. Ask students to identify symbols such as baseball signals (body language indicating that a player is safe or out) or countries' flags. Have groups of students draw symbols and explain the meaning of each. Provide art supplies for making symbols or provide posters that show symbols created by body language.

"Noah's Ark"

After reading books related to the story of Noah's ark such as *Prayers from the Ark*, have students select one of the following ways to respond to the books: (1) Make an ark from craft sticks and make animals for the ark out of pipe cleaners on clay, (2) Make a mural of the voyage, (3) Make a diorama showing the animals and the ark, or (4) Make a puppet stage shaped like an ark with portholes for the puppets, make pairs of animal puppets, and write a short skit in which each animal discusses life on the ark. Provide the art supplies needed for each activity and assist students with the projects. Display the first three projects in the reading center. Have the puppet show presented to the entire class.

"Rainy Days"

Share the book *One Wide River to Cross* with the class. Ask students to identify songs related to rain. Sing some rainy day songs. As the class sings, make rain sounds by having one group of students rub their hands together, another group snap their fingers, and a third group slap their legs.

Bulletin Boards

"Animals on the Ark"

Design and create a bulletin board with a large ark in the center. Have students select an animal and draw a picture of that animal on the ark. Each student can write or dictate a story or poem similar to those in *Prayers from the Ark*. Display pictures and stories around the bulletin board.

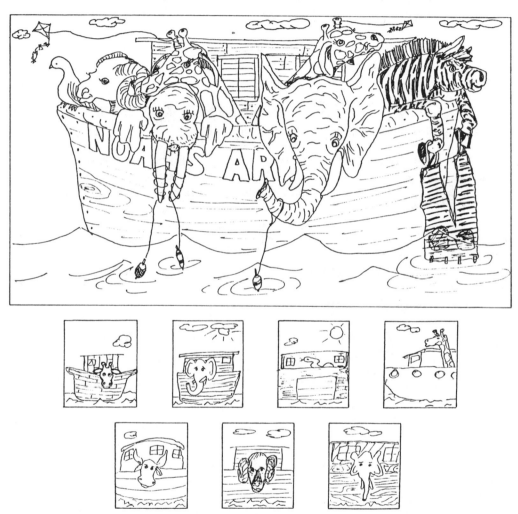

"Animal Homes"

Place the heading Animal Homes on the bulletin board with five subheadings: Pond/Ocean, Desert, Sky, Forest/Woodlands, and North or South Pole. Have students place the picture and paragraphs they wrote after the visit to the zoo (as part of the science activity "Where Do Animals Live?") under the proper heading on the bulletin board.

Related Books

Brenner, Barbara. *Noah and the Flood*. Illustrated by Annie Mitra. New York: Bantam Doubleday Dell (Bantam Books), 1992.
　　The story of Noah and the flood.

Day, David. *Aska's Animals*. Illustrated by Warabé Aska. New York: Bantam Doubleday Dell (Doubleday), 1991.
　　Poems feature animals from around the world.

de Gasztold, Carmen. Translated by Rumer Godden. *Prayers from the Ark*.
　　Illustrated by Barry Moses. New York: Viking, 1992.
　　The poems feature animals on Noah's ark.

Ehlert, Lois. *Color Zoo*. New York: J. B. Lippincott, 1989. (Caldecott Honor)
　　Zoo animals are produced by manipulating shapes and colors.

Emberly, Barbara. *One Wide River to Cross*. Illustrated by Ed Emberly. Boston: Little, Brown, 1966.
　　(Caldecott Honor)
　　The picture book is an adaptation of an African-American spiritual about Noah and the flood.

Gibbons, Gail. *Weather Forecasting*. Illustrated by the author. New York: Four Winds Press, 1987.
　　Weather forecasting for the four seasons is clearly explained with bright illustrations.

Graham, Lorenz. *God Wash the World and Start Again*. Illustrated by Clare Ross. New York: Thomas Y. Crowell, 1971.
　　An African version of Noah's ark is told in this book.

Haley, Gail E. *Noah's Ark*. Illustrated by the author. New York: Atheneum, 1971.
　　This modern version contains pairs of all animals except the ostrich.

Haywood, Linda. *Noah's Ark*. Illustrated by Freire Wright. New York: Random Books for Young Readers, 1987.
　　The familiar story is retold for young readers.

Hoban, Tana. *A Children's Zoo*. Photographs by the author. New York: Greenwillow Books, 1985.
　　Zoo animals are described through words and photographs with a glossary that includes animal habitats and eating habits.

———. *Is It Larger? Is It Smaller?* Photographs by the author. New York: Greenwillow Books, 1985.
　　Photographs are used to present the concept of size.

Hogrogian, Nonny. *Noah's Ark*. Illustrated by the author. New York: Knopf Books for Young Readers, 1986.
　　This version of the story of Noah's ark follows the biblical tale.

Holl, Adelaide. *The Rain Puddle*. Illustrated by Roger Duvoisin. New York: Lothrop, Lee & Shepard, 1965.
　　Animals are confused by looking in a rain puddle.

Hopkins, Lee Bennett, selected by. *To the Zoo: Animal Poems*. Illustrated by John Wallner. Boston: Little, Brown, 1992.
This is a beautifully illustrated book of poems about the animals in the zoo.

Hutton, Warwick. *Noah and the Great Flood*. New York: Atheneum, 1977.
Words and pictures are used to tell the story of the flood.

Johnston, Ginny, and Judy Cutchins. *Windows on Wildlife*. New York: Morrow Junior Books, 1990.
This information book shows how realistic habitats for plants and animals are designed for zoos, wildlife parks, and aquariums.

Kalan, Robert. *Rain*. Illustrated by Donald Crews. New York: Mulberry Books, 1978.
The illustrations describe a rain storm.

Machotka, Hana. *What Neat Feet*! New York: Morrow Junior Books, 1991.
This book describes the feet of various animals and show how they help the animals survive.

McMillan, Bruce. *Becca Backward, Becca Frontward*. New York: Lothrop, Lee & Shepard, 1986.
Photographs are used to demonstrate the concepts presented in the book.

Prelutsky, Jack. *Rainy, Rainy Saturday*. Illustrated by Marilyn Hafner. New York: Greenwillow Books, 1980.
This book of poetry contains fourteen poems about rain.

Rounds, Glen. *Washday on Noah's Ark*. Illustrated by the author. New York: Holiday House, 1991.
A modern version of Noah and his ark told as a tall tale.

Scheer, Julian. *Rain Makes Applesauce*. Illustrated by Marvin Bilech. New York: Holiday House, 1964. (Caldecott Honor)
Humorous pictures present a series of silly statements about rainfall.

Spier, Peter. *Fast-Slow, High-Low: A Book of Opposites*. Illustrated by the author. New York: Doubleday, 1973.
Opposite concepts are introduced in this picture book.

———. *Noah's Ark*. Illustrated by the author. Garden City, N.Y.: Doubleday, 1977.
Detailed color illustrations of building the ark, the adventures aboard the ark, and beginning life after the Flood.

———. *Peter Spier's Rain*. New York: Doubleday, 1982.
The pictures tell of two children's experiences in the rain.

Stevenson, James. *We Hate Rain!* New York: Greenwillow Books, 1988.
This adventure develops as a grandfather entertains two bored children with a tall tale about a flood.

Tresselt, Alvin. *Rain Drop Splash!* Pictures by Leonard Weisgard. New York: Mulberry Books, 1990.
This book follows rain from small bodies of water to the sea.

Yektai, Niki. *Bears in Pairs*. Illustrated by Diane DeGroat. New York: Macmillan, 1991.
This is a beginning reader's rhyming text about pairs of bears on their way to a party.

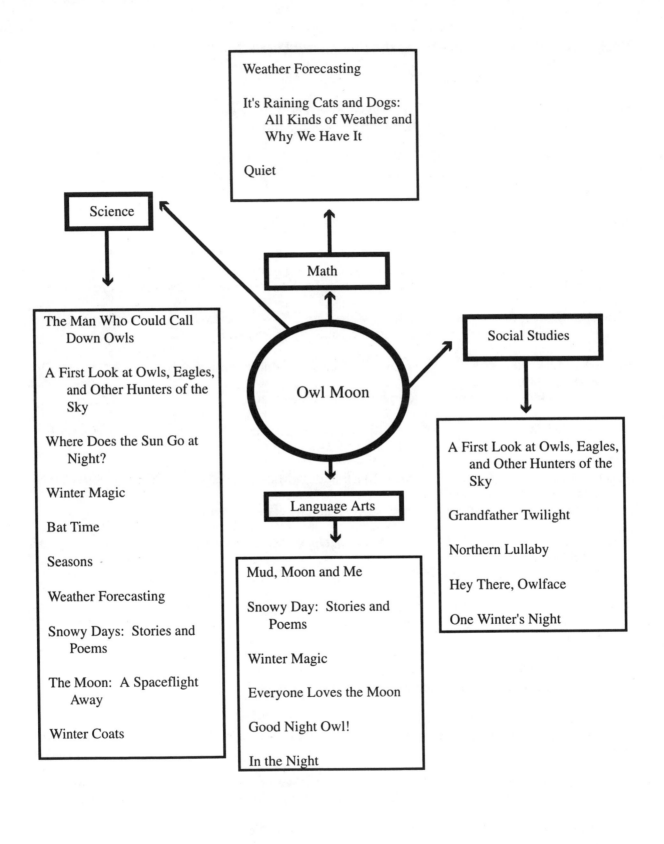

Weather Forecasting

It's Raining Cats and Dogs:
    All Kinds of Weather and
    Why We Have It

Quiet

Science

Math

Social Studies

**The Man Who Could Call
Down Owls**

**A First Look at Owls, Eagles,
and Other Hunters of the
Sky**

**Where Does the Sun Go at
Night?**

Winter Magic

Bat Time

Seasons

Weather Forecasting

**Snowy Days: Stories and
Poems**

**The Moon: A Spaceflight
Away**

Winter Coats

Owl Moon

Language Arts

Mud, Moon and Me

Snowy Day: Stories and
    Poems

Winter Magic

Everyone Loves the Moon

Good Night Owl!

In the Night

A First Look at Owls, Eagles,
    and Other Hunters of the
    Sky

Grandfather Twilight

Northern Lullaby

Hey There, Owlface

One Winter's Night

4

Owl Moon

ॐ

Yolen, Jane. *Owl Moon*. Illustrated by John Schoenherr. New York: Philomel, 1987. (Caldecott Medal)

Genre: Picture book

Summary: Beautiful illustrations of a snow-covered landscape enhance the text revealing a young girl's relationship with her father and with nature as they silently walk through the dark woods in search of an owl.

Content Areas: Language arts, math, science, social studies, and creative arts. This book could be used to introduce a science unit on nature.

Brainstorming Starters:

Owl	Flashlight
Owling	Statue
Nature	Winter coat
Landscape	Mitten
Silent	Scarf
Dark woods	Brave
Hoot	Relationships
Moonlight	

Activities for Language Arts

"Poems"

Display several books of poetry, including *Mud, Moon and Me*; *Snowy Day: Stories and Poems*; *Winter Magic*; *Everyone Loves the Moon*; and *In the Night*. Read several poems from the books. Have students write poems about winter, birds, owls, animals, or an adventure with a friend or family members. Collect the poems in a booklet of favorite class poems and place it on the reading table.

"Owl Moon Dictionary"

Brainstorm to find out what students know about owls, winter nights, and adventures. After reading *Owl Moon* and *Good Night, Owl!*, develop a list of vocabulary terms or words associated with the topics. Working in small groups, have each student compile a dictionary by illustrating each word with pictures or a sentence. The completed assignment is a dictionary of words related to owls.

Activities for Math

"Weather Maps"

After examining two books on weather, *Weather Forecasting* and *It's Raining Cats and Dogs: All Kinds of Weather and Why We Have It*, ask students to describe the weather conditions of the day. Discuss how the weather changes during a day. Provide a videotape or watch a current weather report on a television set. Pass out newspaper pages containing the weather report and have students study the weather map. Introduce symbols used on weather maps and television weather reports.

Furnish a large map and weather symbols. Have students pretend to control the weather by placing symbols on the map. Compare these maps with the newspaper weather map.

Show the students a thermometer and have them explain its purpose. Allow volunteers to read the temperature. Place a thermometer outside the classroom window. Give each student a chart to record the temperature each morning and afternoon. Record the temperature at specific times during the day. Have students note changes by placing a plus sign or minus sign after each reading to indicate whether there was an increase or decrease from the day before. At the end of the week, have students compare the temperatures they recorded by comparing the number of plus or minus signs. Have students work in pairs to compare their findings. If there are differences, help the students find the error.

"One Minute"

Show students a clock. Discuss minutes and how many are in an hour. Show how the movement of the clock's hands mark the minutes and hours. Have students list things that can be done in one minute, such as putting on shoes or brushing teeth. Compare the lists. After reading *Quiet*, have students remain silent for one minute and then for two minutes. Allow students to describe how long each period seemed. Set a timer for ten minutes to show students this time frame. Proceed with regular class activities as the timer runs. After the ten-minute period, have the students list all of the things they were able to do during the period of time.

Activities for Science

"Predator/Prey"

After reading *The Man Who Could Call Down Owls* and *A First Look at Owls, Eagles, and Other Hunters of the Sky*, invite a resource person to speak to the class about how to take care of injured and endangered owls and other birds. After the talk, have students role-play what to do if an injured owl or bird is found. After the role-playing activity, show pictures of various owls. Ask the students to describe them by coloring and size. Ask students to brainstorm a list of foods that owls eat and where they might find the food. Introduce the owl as a consumer of food and as a predator and a prey. Discuss the predator–prey relationship in the food chain. Have students think of other animals that are either predators or prey. Ask students to collect pictures of owls, birds, and animals. Have students work cooperatively to classify owls by whether or not they are endangered. A good reference would be the wildlife conservation section of an encyclopedia.

"Nocturnal Animals"

Share the books *Where Does the Sun Go at Night?*; *Winter Magic*; and *Bat Time*. Ask students to think about nighttime activities or things that occur only at night. Introduce the owl as a nocturnal animal. On the chalkboard make a list of other nocturnal animals suggested by the students. Divide the class into groups to research the habits and behavior of nocturnal animals. Have each group make charts showing the nocturnal behavior of various animals. Display the charts and compare the groups' findings. Have the groups draw a nighttime picture of a selected animal.

"Seasons"

Have students describe the weather in *Owl Moon*; *Seasons*; *Weather Forecasting*; *Snowy Day: Stories and Poems*; and *Winter Coats*. Use a calendar to divide the months by season. Provide pictures of various sports or activities and have students match the pictures with the appropriate seasons (i.e., harvesting in the fall, swimming in the summer, and so forth). Have students describe activities that can be done only in cold weather. Divide the class into four groups. Assign each group one season. Have the groups draw pictures of activities that can be done and clothing that can be worn during the assigned seasons. Each group's work can be shared with the class.

"Moon Phases"

After reading *Owl Moon* and *The Moon: A Spaceflight Away*, ask students to describe the moon in each story and tell how it influenced the events in that story. Use a flashlight and globe to demonstrate the rotation of the earth and how this creates night and day. Allow volunteers to demonstrate the rotation. Ask students to list the differences in night and day; discuss their suggestions. Introduce the position of the moon as it moves in orbit around the earth. Use the flashlight, globe, and a ball to demonstrate how the features of the moon change as it orbits around the earth. Hold the ball between an inflatable world and flashlight. Have students observe the lighted surface. Move the ball to the other three positions around the globe and keep the globe in the same position. Have students observe the ball by looking over the globe for the lighted surface. Identify the new moon, first quarter, full moon, and last quarter by repeating the procedure.

This may also be illustrated by moving the moon to various positions around the earth on a gear-driven orbiter/planetarium model (such models are available from school supply companies). Introduce the name of the moon phases with overhead transparencies or pictures (see page 32).

Give students a calendar of the current month showing the moon phases and a calendar that has no moon phases. Have students label the blank calendar with the moon phases by drawing them in on the appropriate days. Let students take the calendars home to view the moon. Encourage students to record what they see in their journals.

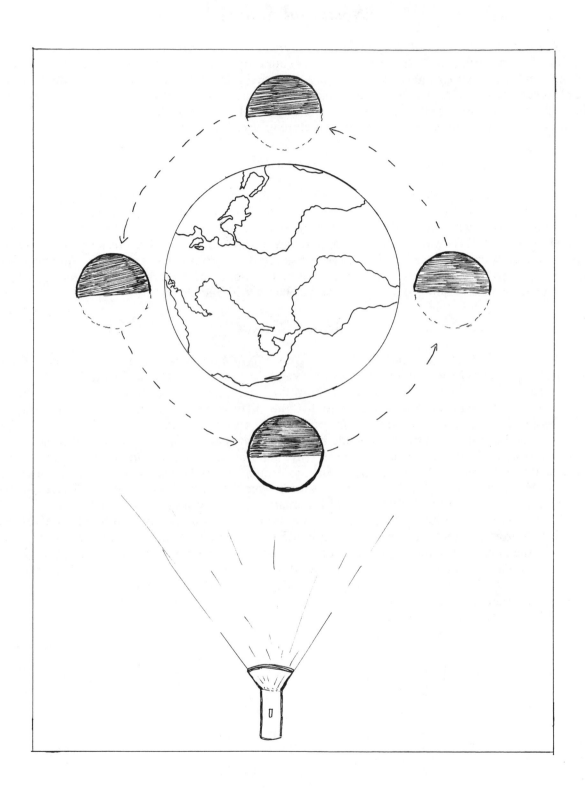

Activities for Social Studies

"Field Trip"

After reading *Owl Moon* and *A First Look at Owls, Eagles and Other Hunters of the Sky,* plan a field trip to an aviary, zoo, or museum to view birds. Have students compile a number of questions to ask and things to look for on the trip. Before the field trip, divide the class into groups for viewing certain birds and finding out three things about the assigned birds. Make each group responsible for reporting back on its birds. After returning from the field trip, have students discuss what they saw, the questions that were answered, and what new things they learned. Have the students listen to an audiotape of owl and other bird sounds. Encourage the students to identify various owl sounds and let volunteers make owl sounds.

"Adventure Stories"

Read *Owl Moon*; *Grandfather Twilight*; *One Winter's Night*; *Northern Lullaby*; and *Hey There, Owlface* to the class. After listening to the stories with their eyes closed, have students describe scenes from the stories and describe how the descriptions of the weather made them feel. Have the students tell the stories from an owl's perspective. Following the discussion, ask students, "Have you ever had an adventure like this one?" Have students draw pictures about an adventure they have had. Each student can write about the pictures, share them with another student, or tell the teacher about the adventure.

Activities for Creative Arts

"Owl Sounds"

Listen to recordings of bird and owl sounds. Identify the owl or bird making the sounds. Sing "Old MacDonald" using bird calls of different birds and owls instead of farm animals.

"Owl Moon Diorama"

After reading *Owl Moon,* have the students create a diorama about the book. Provide materials, such as a box, construction paper, glue, scissors, paints, cotton balls, and pictures. Divide the class into three committees: an animal and people committee, an environment committee, and a moon committee. Have each committee contribute to the development of the diorama. When the diorama is complete, create a display featuring the diorama, books, and posters.

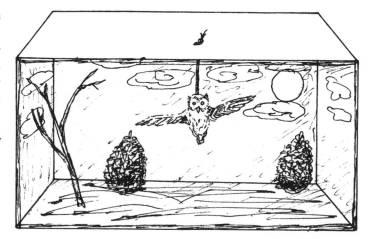

"Picture Books"

Provide materials for painting pictures, including tempera paints, paper, brushes, and pictures of various owls and birds. Students can paint several pictures of birds and owls, label each picture with the name of the bird or owl and a brief description, and compile the pages to make a picture book. The title page should feature the name of the student artist. The completed books can be placed on the library table for sharing.

Bulletin Boards

"Clothing"

Make a bulletin board with the theme of the types of clothes we wear for each season of the year. Use committees for each season. Dress paper dolls appropriately. Place a table in front of the bulletin board and encourage students to display stuffed animals, dolls, or action figures dressed for different seasons.

"Owls"

Create a bulletin board that features various kinds of owls. Supply students with pictures of owls to identify. Have a committee prepare the background of the bulletin board by painting a mural of a night scene. Write a heading at the top of the bulletin board. Have another group paste the owl pictures on construction paper and label each picture. Glue the pictures on the mural.

Related Books

Dates, Betty. *Hey There, Owlface*. Illustrated by Leslie Morrill. New York: Holiday House, 1991
A boy reacts when one of two owls he has watched in a barn is shot.

Bauer, Caroline F., ed. *Snowy Day: Stories and Poems*. Illustrated by Margot Tomes. New York: J. B. Lippincott, 1986.
Stories and poems by recognized authors, easy recipes and crafts, snow trivia, and black-and-white sketches depict the winter season.

Berger, Barbara. *Grandfather Twilight*. New York: Philomel, 1984.
This book reveals how Grandfather Twilight goes about the task of bringing night.

Branley, Franklyn M. *It's Raining Cats and Dogs: All Kinds of Weather and Why We Have It*. Illustrated by True Kelley. Boston: Houghton Mifflin, 1987.
This information book offers folklore and information about rain, snow, smog, lightning, hurricanes, tornadoes, and clouds.

Bunting, Eve. *The Man Who Could Call Down Owls*. Illustrated by Charles Mikolaycak. New York: Macmillan, 1984.
This read-aloud book tells of a wise old man who had a special relationship with owls. The book includes descriptions of several types of owls.

Carlstrom, Nancy W. *Northern Lullaby*. Illustrated by Leo Dillon and Diane Dillon. New York: Putnam (Philomel), 1992.
A child says good night to the Alaskan winter scene.

Darling, David. *The Moon: A Spaceflight Away*. Illustrated by Jeanette Swofford. Minneapolis, Minn.: Dillon, 1984.
The book describes the moon and its functions.

Gibbons, Gail. *Weather Forecasting*. Illustrated by the author. New York: Four Winds Press, 1987.
This brightly illustrated book tells about weather and forecasting during the four seasons.

Ginsburg, Mirra. *Where Does the Sun Go at Night?* Pictures by Jose Aruego and Ariane Dewey. New York: Mulberry Books, 1981.
This book depicts the sun as a person with a family that takes care of him at night.

Goennel, Heidi. *Seasons*. Illustrated by the author. Waltham, Mass.: Little, Brown, 1986.
This simple picture book describes each season.

Hasler, Eveline. *Winter Magic*. Illustrated by Michele Lemieux. Minneapolis, Minn.: William Morrow, 1984.
Poetic words and pictures describe a midnight adventure of a boy and his cat during the winter.

Horowitz, Tuth. *Bat Time*. Illustrated by Susan Avishai. Riverside, N.J.: Four Winds Press, 1991.
A young girl and her father share a nightly ritual of watching bats eat insects.

Hutchins, Pat. *Good Night, Owl!* Illustrated by the author. New York: Macmillan, 1972.
 This beautifully illustrated book shows all the animals in the forest that keep owl awake.

Lockwood, Primrose. *One Winter's Night*. Illustrated by Elaine Mills. New York: Macmillan, 1991.
 Joseph's father ventures out on a cold, moonlit night and brings home a puppy.

Mason, Margo. *Winter Coats*. Illustrated by Laura Rader. Des Plaines, Ill.: Bantam Books, 1989.
 This book describes the differences in the winter clothes of people and animals.

Parnall, Peter. *Quiet*. Illustrated by the author. New York: Morrow Junior Books, 1989.
 A boy spends a silent time in a meadow.

Selsam, Millicent E., and Joyce Hunt. *A First Look at Owls, Eagles, and Other Hunters of the Sky*.
 Illustrated by Harriett Springer. New York: Walker, 1986.
 This is an informational book that answers in detail questions about birds of prey.

Shipton, Jonathan. *In the Night*. Illustrated by Gill Scriven. Boston: Little, Brown, 1987.
 A poetic text captures the mysterious magic of the night.

Weil, Zaro. *Mud, Moon and Me*. Illustrated by Jo Burroughs. Boston: Houghton Mifflin, 1992.
 A collection of imaginative poems for young readers.

Yolen, Jane. *Owl Moon*. Illustrated by John Schoenherr. New York: Philomel, 1987.
 Beautiful illustrations of a snow-covered landscape enhance the text revealing a young girl's relationship with her father and with nature as they silently walk through the dark woods in search of an owl.

Young, James. *Everyone Loves the Moon*. Boston: Little, Brown, 1991.
 This is a charming story, told in rhymes, about Mr. Raccoon trying to persuade Ms. Possum to love both him and the moon.

Supplemental Reading

Aliki. *The Two of Them*. Illustrated by the author. New York: Greenwillow Books, 1979.
 The love of a grandfather and granddaughter is shown through colors and pictures.

Anderson, Lena. *Stina*. New York: Greenwillow Books, 1989.
 A girl's summer visit on an island with her grandfather is told.

Hines, Anna G. *Moon's Wish*. Illustrated by the author. New York: Clarion Books, 1992.
 A young girl asks the moon to make a wish.

Mitra, Annie. *Penguin Moon*. Illustrated by the author. New York: Holiday House, 1989.
 A penguin talks with the moon.

Ormerod, Jan. *Moonlight*. Illustrated by the author. New York: Lothrop, Lee & Shepard, 1982.
 A wordless picture book about a nighttime ritual.

San Souci, Daniel. *North Country Night*. Illustrated by the author. New York: Doubleday, 1990.
 Animals are shown in pictures.

Spier, Peter. *The Fox Went Out on a Chilly Night*. New York: Doubleday, 1961. (Caldecott Honor)
    A picture book based on the animal folktale.

Tejima. *Owl Lake*. Illustrated by the author. East Rutherford, N.J.: Philomel, 1987.
    Tejima depicts the nocturnal activities of an owl family through beautiful woodcuts.

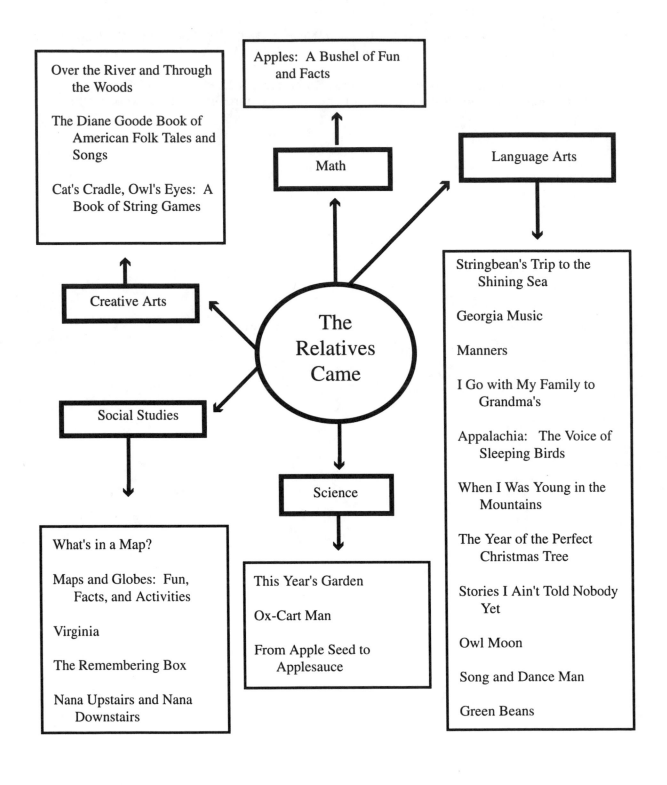

Over the River and Through the Woods

The Diane Goode Book of American Folk Tales and Songs

Cat's Cradle, Owl's Eyes: A Book of String Games

Apples: A Bushel of Fun and Facts

Math

Language Arts

Creative Arts

The Relatives Came

Stringbean's Trip to the Shining Sea

Georgia Music

Manners

I Go with My Family to Grandma's

Appalachia: The Voice of Sleeping Birds

When I Was Young in the Mountains

The Year of the Perfect Christmas Tree

Stories I Ain't Told Nobody Yet

Owl Moon

Song and Dance Man

Green Beans

Social Studies

Science

What's in a Map?

Maps and Globes: Fun, Facts, and Activities

Virginia

The Remembering Box

Nana Upstairs and Nana Downstairs

This Year's Garden

Ox-Cart Man

From Apple Seed to Applesauce

5

The Relatives Came

Rylant, Cynthia. *The Relatives Came*. Illustrated by Stephen Gammell. New York: Bradbury Press, 1985. (Caldecott Honor)

Genre: Contemporary fiction

Summary: The relatives from Virginia came to visit, and everyone had a wonderful time eating, playing, working, singing, and sleeping as one huge, happy family.

Content Areas: Language arts, math, science, social studies, and creative arts. The web developed around this book can be used to introduce a social studies unit on Appalachia or on the importance of family and friends.

Brainstorming Starters:

Feelings	Modes of transportation available today
Mountains	Modes of transportation available in the nineteenth century
Mountain music	Source of night and day
State of Virginia	Source of food on the grocer's shelves
Families	Growing season
Family trees	Grapes
Family members' visits	

Activities for Language Arts

"Family Newsletter"

After reading *The Relatives Came*, *Stringbean's Trip to the Shining Sea*, and *Georgia Music*, have students think about information they would like to share with their relatives. Give each student an outline telling them how to place information on a chart as they think of ideas to share about their immediate family. The information on the chart can be grouped by topics such as the number of people in the family, the name of the family members, ages of family members, roles of the family members, and interesting facts or recent accomplishments about each member of the immediate family. After completing the charts, have students add several members of their extended families to their charts. Explain that the chart can serve as a fact sheet for a newsletter about each family. If computers are available, use them to design and compose the newsletters. If computers are not available, provide a handwritten newsletter as a model. Stress neat handwriting for students not using a computer. Provide assistance to those having difficulty with design or content. Divide the class into small groups to share their newsletters. After the newsletters have been shared in groups, display them on the bulletin board for several days before allowing students to take them home to share with family members.

"Family Stories"

Display related books (see this chapter's bibliography) for students to read. Have students keep reading logs. Allow students who have read *Green Beans, Owl Moon, Manners, I Go with My Family to Grandma's,* and *Song and Dance Man* describe the stories and share their personal responses to the books. Ask students to respond to questions such as, "Have you had visitors recently?" and "What kind of manners do you use when company comes to visit?" Ask students to volunteer to tell a favorite story about when someone came to visit. Ask the students to tell the city and state from which the visitor came. List the various locations on the chalkboard and find them on a map. Encourage students to write a story or draw a picture about a special family member or pet. Compile the stories and pictures into a class book of family stories or place the individual projects on the bulletin board.

"Stories from the Mountains"

After reading *Appalachia: The Voice of Sleeping Birds, When I Was Young in the Mountains, The Year of the Perfect Christmas Tree,* and *Stories I Ain't Told Nobody Yet,* ask students if any of them have ever been to a mountain. List the names of the mountains or mountain ranges visited on the chalkboard. Have volunteers locate the mountains on a map of the United States. Make a chart showing which students have been to various mountains by having students write their names under the mountains they have visited. Allow those who have never been to a mountain to select a mountain that they would like to visit. Divide the class into small groups to compile lists of words that describe mountains. Ask each student to use the group's descriptive words as a guide to drawing a picture about a real or imagined visit to the mountain. Encourage the students to write about their pictures. Display the pictures and stories in the classroom.

Activities for Math

"Measuring Distance"

Use the map key to show how miles are measured on a map (see page 41). Provide the class with a simple outline map of the United States. Have each student use the map key to estimate the distance from where they live to Virginia. Assist those needing help using the map key. Compare the estimates made by class members.

"Measuring with Cooking Utensils"

Provide the students with the opportunity to practice measurement using cooking utensils. Read *Apples: A Bushel of Fun and Facts.* Ask students to identify the words in the recipes that refer to measuring or cooking utensils. Have students collect pictures of the ingredients needed to make apple or grape jelly. Provide the class with a food scale, measuring cups, spoons, containers of various sizes, water, sand, beans, and other materials to measure. Fill various containers with the same quantity (i.e., one cup) of various materials for comparison. Measure out the amounts of liquids and solids called for in various recipes to show volume and weight. For example, compare the weights of one cup of water and one cup of apples. After completing the experiment, have the students create recipes using apples. These can be displayed in a class apple-recipe booklet.

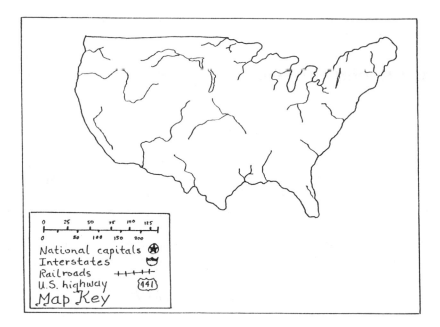

Activities for Science

"Growing Season"

Share *This Year's Garden* and *Ox-Cart Man* with the class. Display a collection of farm pictures that depicts the seasons of the year. Have the students name the seasons and provide facts about each one. Ask them to look at the pictures and identify which season is pictured. Provide materials, such as magazines, for students to find pictures of farm chores. Display the pictures and allow students to tell how farm chores change with the seasons. Divide the class into groups and have each group make a booklet that shows what happens on the farm during the growing season. Place the completed booklets in the science center for sharing.

"Mountains"

After reading the books on Appalachia, have students identify and locate on maps other mountain ranges located in the United States. Have groups of students research various mountain ranges in encyclopedias and trade books. Have each group record facts about the mountains on posters. Compare posters to identify the differences between the Rocky Mountains and the Appalachian Mountains. Display the posters in the classroom.

"Apples"

After reading *From Apple Seed to Applesauce,* show a number of varieties of apples. Tell students the name of each kind of apple. (If the fruit itself is not available, show pictures of different varieties.) Brainstorm the uses of apples and what can be made from apples. Make a chart showing ways apples can be served, such as apple juice, apple pie, and apple butter. Have groups of students research apples, with one group finding information about where they are grown and the current price, another locating recipes using apples, a third group finding pictures of apples and apple products, and a fourth group making applesauce. Serve the applesauce to the class. Give students an apple cut from construction paper and have them write on it one fact about apples. Place these on a tree made from green butcher paper.

Activities for Social Studies

"Family Trees"

Read *The Remembering Box* and *Nana Upstairs and Nana Downstairs*. Give each student a blank family tree. Ask students to fill in the names of the members of their immediate and extended families. Have them take the project home if they need help completing it. After all of the family trees have been returned to class, make a tree out of construction paper for each student. Have the students put the names of their family members on it, starting with grandparents at the trunk of the tree and adding others to the limbs of the tree. Draw a large "class tree" on butcher paper and hang it on a wall of the classroom. Hang the family trees on the class tree.

"Developing Map Skills"

Use the books *What's in a Map?* and *Maps and Globes: Fun, Facts, and Activities* to introduce the concepts related to reading and using maps. After determining what information is in the map keys, review terms related to maps, such as north, south, east, and west. Have students discuss the need for a map to be labeled.

Ask students to identify which state the relatives came from in *The Relatives Came*. Read the book *Virginia* and provide pictures, information, and a large map of Virginia. In small groups, have students use a state map to find the location of their city. Provide each group with a map of the United States. Have a representative from each group select a piece of paper on which you have written the name of a city in Virginia. Have each group plan a trip from their home to the city in Virginia. After marking the route on the map, the group should estimate the distance using the scale of miles on the map key. Have each group record its destination and the mileage estimate on a chart on the chalkboard. Then have each group select a piece of paper on which you have written the name of a city in the United States. Have each group plan the route to this location. Record the mileage estimate for this trip on another chart on the chalkboard. Brainstorm means of transportation to these cities. Write the modes of transportation on slips of paper and have each group select one. Have each group write a collaborative story about a trip to the selected city by the selected mode of transportation. Each group can share its story with the class.

Activities for Creative Arts

"Traveling Songs"

Share *Over the River and Through the Woods* and *The Diane Goode Book of American Folk Tales and Songs* with the class. Provide the class with the opportunity to learn songs from these books. Have students identify songs they can remember singing in the car on family trips. Divide the class into groups to make up songs that can be used to provide entertainment on a trip. These can be shared with the class.

"String Games"

Demonstrate some of the finger games from *Cat's Cradle, Owl's Eyes: A Book of String Games.* Provide string for doing some of the activities in the booklets. Divide the class into groups for practicing. Provide assistance as needed. Each group can share its games with the class.

Bulletin Boards

"Family Tree Stories"
Put a large tree in the middle of the bulletin board under the heading *Family Tree Stories.* Stories written during the language arts activity "Family Stories" can be mounted on construction paper and placed on the tree.

"Appalachia"
Create a bulletin board entitled *Appalachia.* Outline the shape of the Appalachian region and place the map on the bulletin board. Display facts learned about the region around the map. Have students select a place in Appalachia and identify it on the map by placing a pushpin at the appropriate location and writing the name of the place beside the pin.

Related Books

Ackerman, Karen. *Song and Dance Man.* Illustrated by Stephen Gammell. New York: Alfred A. Knopf, 1988. (Caldecott Medal)
   Grandpa shows some of the songs, dances, and jokes from his vaudeville act.

Aliki. *Manners.* Illustrated by the author. New York: Greenwillow Books, 1990.
   This book gives examples of good manners and bad manners.

Arnold, Caroline. *Maps and Globes: Fun, Facts, and Activities.* New York: Franklin Watts, 1984.
   This information book explains the uses of maps and globes with instructions for projects, such as making a balloon globe, a model room, and a giant compass.

Carpenter, Allan. *Virginia.* Illustrated with photographs. Chicago: Children's Press, 1967.
   A pictorial description gives facts about the state of Virginia.

Carson, Jo. *Stories I Ain't Told Nobody Yet.* Chicago: Orchard Books, 1989.
   A collection of Appalachian tales are in this book.

Cartwright, Sally. *What's in a Map?* New York: Putnam, 1976.
   Children are shown how to map their world using blocks, paper and pencil, and their imaginations.

Child, Lydia Maria. *Over the River and Through the Woods*. Illustrated by Brinton Turkle. New York: Putnam, 1984.
This classic song, first published in 1844, is treasured by young and old alike.

Clifford, Eth. *The Remembering Box*. Illustrated by Donna Diamond. Boston: Houghton Mifflin, 1985.
Joshua's grandmother's small objects from her Remembering Box help him understand his Jewish roots.

DePaola, Tomie. *Nana Upstairs and Nana Downstairs*. New York: Putnam, 1973.
This is the story of a boy's relationships with his grandmother and great-grandmother.

Durall, Ann, collector. *The Diane Goode Book of American Folk Tales and Songs*. Illustrated by Diane Goode. New York: E. P. Dutton, 1989.
This is a collection of traditional folk materials.

Griffith, Helen V. *Georgia Music*. Illustrated by James Stevenson. New York: Mulberry Books, 1986.
A little girl and her grandfather share music and nature.

Gryski, Camilla. *Cat's Cradle, Owl's Eyes: A Book of String Games*. Illustrated by Tom Sankey. New York: Beech Tree Books, 1983.
This book gives basic instructions for making string games.

Hall, Donald. *Ox-Cart Man*. Illustrated by Barbara Cooney. New York: Viking, 1979.
A family makes things to sell at the Portsmouth Market.

Houston, Gloria. *The Year of the Perfect Christmas Tree*. Illustrated by Barbara Cooney. New York: Dial Press, 1988.
After Father goes to war, a small girl and her mother provide the perfect Christmas tree for the village church.

Hunt, Bernice K. *Apples: A Bushel of Fun and Facts*. Illustrated by Roland Rodegast. New York: Parents, 1976.
This information book covers the cultivation, grafting, and development of apple trees, as well as a variety of apples and some recipes.

Johnson, Hannah Lyons. *From Apple Seed to Applesauce*. Illustrated with photographs. New York: Lothrop, Lee & Shepard, 1977.
This information book covers apples, from growing them to their uses.

Levinson, Riki. *I Go with My Family to Grandma's*. Illustrated by Diane Goode. New York: E. P. Dutton, 1986.
Five families of cousins arrive by different means of transportation at Grandma's house during the early 1900s.

Rylant, Cynthia. *Appalachia: The Voice of Sleeping Birds*. Illustrated by Barry Moser. San Diego, Calif.: Harcourt Brace Jovanovich, 1991.
Pictures and words make a beautiful connection between the people of Appalachia and their surroundings.

————. *The Relatives Came.* Illustrated by Stephen Gammell. New York: Bradbury Press, 1985.
The relatives from Virginia came to visit, and everyone had a wonderful time eating, playing, working, singing, and sleeping as one huge, happy family.

————. *This Year's Garden.* Pictures by Mary Szilagh. New York: Bradbury Press, 1984.
A family plans its summer garden, harvests the garden, and begins to plan for next year's garden.

————. *When I Was Young in the Mountains.* Illustrated by Diane Goode. New York: E. P. Dutton, 1982.
The author remembers her Appalachian childhood and tells about her busy, peaceful life in her extended family and the community.

Thomas, Elizabeth. *Green Beans.* Illustrated by Vicki Jo Redenbaugh. Minneapolis, Minn.: Carolrhoda Books, 1992.
A young girl and her opinionated grandmother learn to appreciate each other's views.

Williams, Vera B., and Jennifer Williams. *Stringbean's Trip to the Shining Sea.* New York: Greenwillow Books, 1988.
A trip to the West Coast is pictured through postcards.

Yolen, Jane. *Owl Moon.* Illustrated by John Schoenherr. New York: Philomel, 1987. (Caldecott Medal)
A girl and her father take a cold, quiet walk on a moonlit night, looking for an owl.

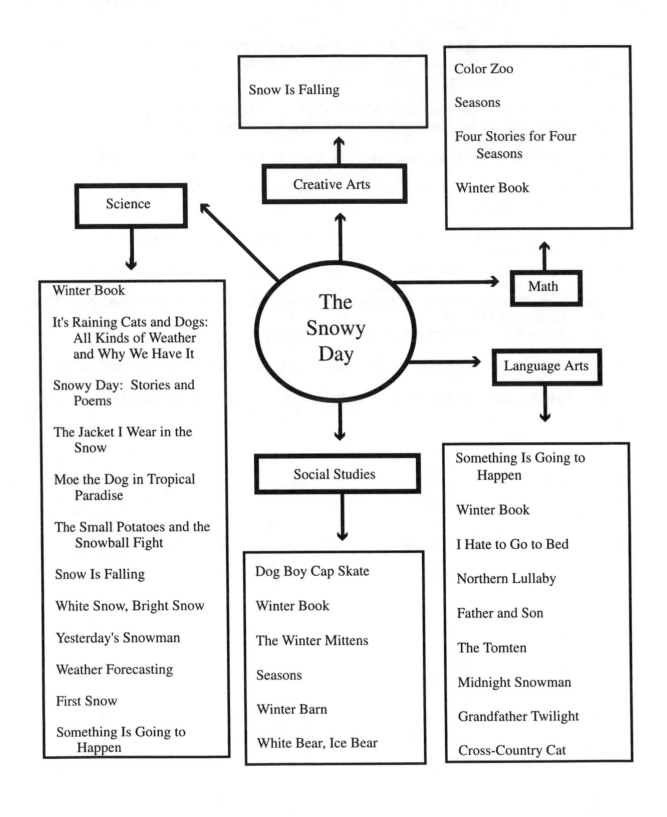

Snow Is Falling

Color Zoo

Seasons

Four Stories for Four Seasons

Winter Book

Creative Arts

Science

Math

The Snowy Day

Language Arts

Winter Book

It's Raining Cats and Dogs: All Kinds of Weather and Why We Have It

Snowy Day: Stories and Poems

The Jacket I Wear in the Snow

Moe the Dog in Tropical Paradise

The Small Potatoes and the Snowball Fight

Snow Is Falling

White Snow, Bright Snow

Yesterday's Snowman

Weather Forecasting

First Snow

Something Is Going to Happen

Social Studies

Dog Boy Cap Skate

Winter Book

The Winter Mittens

Seasons

Winter Barn

White Bear, Ice Bear

Something Is Going to Happen

Winter Book

I Hate to Go to Bed

Northern Lullaby

Father and Son

The Tomten

Midnight Snowman

Grandfather Twilight

Cross-Country Cat

6

The Snowy Day
ॐ

Keats, Ezra Jack. *The Snowy Day*. Illustrated by the author. New York: Viking, 1962. (Caldecott Medal)

Genre: Picture book

Summary: A young black boy delights in his first snowfall.

Content Areas: Language arts, math, science, social studies, and creative arts. This book can be used to introduce a science unit on winter.

Brainstorming Starters:

Snow   Feelings
Snowman   Bedtime
Seasons   Families
Winter sports

Activities for Language Arts

"Listening to Extend the Story"

To prepare for this listening activity, give students sheets of drawing paper, art supplies, and crayons. Ask students to listen as you read and plan to draw pictures that add a new adventure to the end of the story. Read *The Snowy Day* aloud. Have the students close their eyes and try to imagine the story as you read. After reading the story, ask students to think about what the little boys might have done when they went out to play in the snow. Have the students draw a picture or pictures showing the activities of the little boy and his friend playing in the snow. Encourage students to show and explain their pictures to the class. Another book that would enhance this activity is *Something Is Going to Happen*.

"Snowy Day Adventure"

Share *Cross-Country Cat*, *Midnight Snowman*, and *Winter Book* with students. If you live in a climate where it seldom snows, ask the class how many have seen snow. If only a few have seen it, have them describe the experience and how it made them feel. All students can describe snowy-day activities or experiences that they have had or have seen in pictures, such as sledding, building snowmen, making tracks and designs in the snow, feeding birds, and making snow cream. Ask students to list three winter sports. Ask the students to share their lists and record the responses on the chalkboard. After discussing the responses, display several pictures with snowy backgrounds and families involved in winter activities. Ask students to describe how the pictures make them feel. Ask individuals to write stories or draw pictures of real or imagined adventures in the snow. Divide into groups to share the adventure stories. Have the groups compile their members' stories. Provide materials each group can use to make a big book about a snowy day. As books are completed, have groups swap books and read the adventures of another group. Place the finished books in the reading center.

"Nighttime at Home"

Several days before beginning this activity have students take home a note requesting a picture of their family. To begin the activity, share the books, *Grandfather Twilight, I Hate to Go to Bed, Northern Lullaby, Father and Son,* and *The Tomten* with the class. Ask students to describe the main events in the stories and tell how the stories relate to nighttime. After this discussion, have the students show the pictures they brought to school. If some students could not or did not bring a picture, have them draw a picture of their family. Encourage students to discuss the pictures and tell about their family. Ask students if all families are the same in number, ages, shapes, and number of brothers or sisters. Focus the discussion on how families can be very different and have many different experiences and routines. Have the students place the pictures on a bulletin board or in a display area.

Ask students to think about going to bed. Develop a chart of the times that students go to bed. Discuss preparations that must be made before going to bed. Ask students if all families must prepare for going to bed. Brainstorm and list preparations, such as planning a time to go to bed, setting the alarm clock, putting on sleeping clothes, selecting clothing for the next day, reading or being read to, and turning off lights. Ask students whether the routine might differ for different families or for people in other areas or countries. Ask students to describe events, such as a change in the weather (i.e., a snowstorm or icy streets) that disrupted or changed the family routine for going to bed or getting up in the morning.

Have students list two of the ideas shared about families' bedtime routines. Divide the class into groups. Ask each group to select one bedtime activity, such as reading or being told a bedtime story, and role-play the activity for the class. Encourage the students to record their bedtime routines in their journals for several days.

Activities for Math

"Patterns"

Cut several large circles and triangles from styrofoam meat trays. Also cut six circles and six triangles for each student. Divide the class into groups of four or five, and give each group a styrofoam circle and a triangle. Have each group study the circle and triangle for several minutes before telling the class how they would explain the difference in the two shapes to someone who had never seen either shape. Following this activity, display a pattern made up of one circle followed by one triangle, followed by two circles and then two triangles. Ask students to duplicate this design with their shapes. Display a new pattern; have students use the styrofoam forms as stencils to draw the same pattern. Divide into groups. Ask each group to make a set of ten circles and ten triangles from red, green, blue, orange, and purple construction paper with two circles and two triangles of each color. Use five circles and five triangles with magnetic strips on the back to show different patterns. Place a pattern, such as one red circle, two green triangles, and one green circle, on a magnetic board (a cookie sheet will work). Ask the groups to decide what comes next; each group should hold up the appropriate cards in response. Check the response and give additional patterns for the groups to follow.

Break into groups. Provide magazines and have students look for pictures of objects that are round or triangular. After finding many pictures, have the students place the pictures in a pattern on poster board. Have each group share its completed pattern with the class.

Display pictures of snowmen in three sizes, using circles and triangles for the features. Give each group art supplies, such as construction paper, cotton balls and sheeting, buttons, twigs, and fabric, to construct snowmen in three sizes from circles and triangles. The snowmen can be placed on construction paper and attached to the bulletin board. *Color Zoo* would enhance this activity.

"Review Numbers One Through Ten"

Display ten snowmen made from styrofoam balls. Have students make cards for the numbers one through ten. Have the students count the snowmen: Display the first snowman (students say, "One") and add one snowman at a time until all ten are displayed and counted. As they count, have students hold up the appropriate card.

Divide the class into pairs; give each pair a set of ten snowmen cut from construction paper. Each snowman should be decorated with one to ten black dots("pieces of charcoal") to form the mouth, eyes, nose, and buttons on the body. Each snowman should be wearing a hat with three numbers on it; one of the three numbers must correspond with the number of pieces of "charcoal" on the snowman. Have the students take turns counting the pieces of "charcoal" on each snowman and selecting the matching number from the snowman's hat. After each student has counted, give each pair of students arts supplies, including construction paper, cotton, twigs, fabric, and buttons, for making a snowman. Have students make a hat for their snowman and write on the hat the number of buttons used to decorate the snowman. Have the students display their snowmen by attaching them to the chalkboard so that the numbers on the snowmen's hats are in sequence from one to ten.

"Snowy Season"

Display pictures that show activities that occur during the various seasons. Before discussing the pictures, show the class a calendar and ask how many months make up a year. Continue by asking students whether each month has the same number of days, and to name the days of the week. Share *Seasons*, *Four Stories for Four Seasons*, and *Winter Book* with the class. Discuss the books and ask students to identify the season in each of the displayed pictures. Write the words *Spring*, *Summer*, *Fall*, and *Winter* on cards and ask the students to describe each season. List the descriptive words under the correct season and then ask students to name sports or recreational activities that occur during each season. After showing how the calendar can be divided into seasons, have the students count the months in each season. Display a large calendar and point out the months of winter. Divide the class into four groups and assign each group one season. Give each group a calendar that includes only the months for that group's season. Have the students count the number of days in the season. Discuss the number of days in each season. Provide the groups with calendars of the winter season with several dates missing from each month. Ask the students to fill in the blanks and check their work with other members of their group. Give the students a calendar for the current month. Have them highlight the current week. Instruct them to mark off each day of the week by recording a word on the calendar that describes the weather for that day. At the end of the week, have students compare their words for each day.

Activities for Science

"Seasons"

Read the books *It's Raining Cats and Dogs: All Kinds of Weather and Why We Have It, Winter Book* and *Snowy Day: Stories and Poems.* Ask the students to list recreational activities they enjoy. After completing the lists, have the students write beside each activity the season in which one can participate in it. Divide the class into four groups. Assign each group one season. Have each group research additional recreational events and the weather characteristic of the season. Have the research groups compare their findings.

Ask students to think about the four seasons and to select their favorite. Allow students to name their choice and tell why it is their favorite. Ask students, "What would happen if we didn't have winter?" Make a chart of their answers. Have them draw pictures or write about the importance of each season. Have them share their work in small groups and make a booklet for display and later reading.

"Preparing for a Trip"

Place *The Jacket I Wear in the Snow, Moe the Dog in Tropical Paradise,* and *The Small Potatoes and the Snowball Fight* on the reading table. Suggest that students read these in preparation for this activity.

Display a large globe and provide each student with a small world map. Show the two poles on the globe and have students find the two poles on their maps. Have students brainstorm to find out what they know about the equator and how the seasons are opposite in different hemispheres. After clearing up any misunderstandings, have students find on their maps a country that is experiencing the opposite season. Ask students to find out information about the average temperature and weather during the present month of the year in the selected country. Have them check weather reports on the television or in the newspaper or ask the librarian to find the current temperature in the selected country. Have students compare the temperature in the selected country with the local temperature. Have students try to find pictures that show the clothing worn by the native population. Divide the class into groups or pairs to plan a trip to another country. Have each group list what clothing the students will take on the trip. Each group can share its plans and give the rationale for its selections.

"Building a Snowman"

After reading *Snow Is Falling; White Snow, Bright Snow; Yesterday's Snowman; Weather Forecasting; First Snow;* and *Something Is Going to Happen,* have students discuss how snow changes the looks of the city or country. Also have them discuss places you might find a snowman. Ask students to describe steps in making a snowman. Show six pictures of a snowman being built. Give six students the pictures in random order and have them come to the front of the room and stand so that the events in the pictures are in proper sequence. Distribute blank cards (at least three to each student) and have students draw progressive pictures of a snowman being built. When these are completed, have students divide into pairs to sequence their partner's cards and to collect pictures of snowmen being built. The pictures can be shared with the class as different types of snowmen are discussed.

"Melting Snow and Ice"

After reading *Yesterday's Snowman* and *The Snowy Day*, discuss the picture in which the snowball Peter put in his pocket was no longer there. Brainstorm to find out what students know about how snow develops. If the temperature is below freezing outside, take a walk with the children to look for snow-covered or ice-coated trees or bushes. Sprinkle salt on some of the branches and look closely to see if anything happens. In warmer climates, bring ice cubes into the classroom and have the students watch what happens to the ice. Discuss what happened during the experiment.

Have students make two columns on a sheet of paper, with "What I Know About Snow" as one heading and "What I Learned About Snow" as the other heading. Share *Snow Is Falling* with the class and have students look in trade books and science books to find out more about snow. After completing the research, have students share their findings with the class and display their papers on the board.

Activities for Social Studies

"Neighborhood Scenery"

Display pictures of your school or neighborhood during different seasons of the year. Ask students to recall activities that were identified and discussed during the math activity "Snowy Season" and the science activity "Seasons." After recalling activities for each season, have students describe how the looks of the neighborhood change with each season. Suggest reading *Dog Boy Cap Skate*, *Winter Book*, *The Winter Mittens*, and *Seasons* to find out what happens when it snows. Compare the local winter pictures with winter pictures of other locations. List students' ideas of how the areas are alike and how they are different. Divide the class into several groups. Have each student draw four seasonal pictures of his or her neighborhood or house. Display each group's work and have students explain their pictures to the class.

"Winter Adventures"

Have students write a sentence to describe the average weather in your area during the winter months. After sharing the sentences, show pictures of things a family could do during winter months, such as ice skating, skiing, building a snowman, or sledding. Divide into groups. Have each group write a description of a family adventure, such as building a snowman. Draw pictures to illustrate. Display the class stories and pictures in the hallway.

"Caring for Animals in Winter"

Discuss any special plans that must be made for animals during the winter season. Have students list animals that need special provisions during the winter and ways to care for each animal. After sharing the lists, have the class discuss ways various animals prepare for the winter. Read *Winter Barn* and *White Bear, Ice Bear*. Let students discuss any new information gained from these books. In pairs, have students discuss ways to care for household pets during the winter or during a storm. Have each pair list ways to care for pets and share the list with the class. Provide materials and help the class make a bird feeder to be placed outside the classroom window. Assign various students the responsibility of checking the feeder.

Activities for Creative Arts

"Snowflakes"

Look at the pictures of snowflakes in *The Snowy Day* and *Snow Is Falling*. Provide scissors and paper for making snowflakes. Have students make snowflakes from white tissue paper, doilies, or coffee filters. Fold the paper several times to form a triangle and cut shapes out of the top and sides of the paper. Open. Display the snowflakes on the bulletin board.

"Wax Pictures"

Use wax crayons to color a sheet of paper. Use dark blue poster paint to cover the wax crayon. When dry, use craft sticks to scratch the poster paint to make a snow scene. Display these on the bulletin board.

"The Snowy Day Diorama"

Provide shoe boxes or other small boxes, cotton balls and sheeting, construction paper, and other craft materials for making a scene from *The Snowy Day*. Have groups display their dioramas in the science area.

Bulletin Boards

"Changing Seasons"

Make a bulletin board showing how seasons change the neighborhood. Divide the bulletin board into four sections, with each section labeled with a season of the year. Place the heading *Changing Seasons* at the top of the bulletin board. Divide the class into four groups, with each group developing pictures and writing a description of one of the seasons. Display the pictures and descriptions in the appropriate section.

"Winter Scenes"

Cover the bulletin board with white paper and write the heading *Winter Scenes* in the center of the board. Around the edges of the board place the snowflakes that were made in the creative arts activity "Snowflakes." Display the pictures of winter scenes from the creative arts activity "Wax Pictures" on the bulletin board.

Related Books

Arnold, Tim. *The Winter Mittens.* Illustrated by the author. New York: Macmillan (Margaret K. McElderry Books), 1988.
This is a story about human interactions with the seasons.

Barrett, Judi. *I Hate to Go to Bed.* Illustrated by Ray Cruz. New York: Four Winds Press, 1977.
Various humorous excuses are given for not going to sleep.

Bauer, Caroline F. *Midnight Snowman.* Illustrated by Catherine Stock. New York: Atheneum, 1987.
A young girl from a warm climate wishes for snow, and her wish comes true.

Bauer, Caroline F., ed. *Snowy Day: Stories and Poems.* Illustrated by Margot Tomes. New York: J. B. Lippincott, 1986.
Stories and poems by recognized authors, easy recipes and crafts, snow trivia, and black-and-white sketches depict the winter season.

Berger, Barbara. *Grandfather Twilight.* New York: Philomel, 1984.
This book reveals how Grandfather Twilight goes about the task of bringing night.

Branley, Franklyn M. *It's Raining Cats and Dogs: All Kinds of Weather and Why We Have It.* Illustrated by True Kelley. Boston: Houghton Mifflin, 1987.
Information and folklore is given about rain, snow, smog, lightning, hurricanes, tornadoes, and clouds.

———. *Snow Is Falling.* Rev. ed. Illustrated by Holly Keller. New York: Thomas Y. Crowell, 1986.
This book explains how snow can be both helpful and harmful to people, plants, and animals.

Calhoun, Mary. *Cross-Country Cat.* Illustrated by Erick Ingraham. New York: William Morrow, 1979.
A cat who can walk on his hind legs becomes lost and finds his way home on skis.

Carlstrom, Nancy White. *Northern Lullaby.* Illustrated by Leo Dillon and Diane Dillon. New York: Putnam (Philomel), 1992.
A child says good night to the Alaskan winter scene.

dePaola, Tomie. *Four Stories for Four Seasons.* Illustrated by the author. New York: Prentice Hall Press, 1977.
Dog, Cat, Frog, and Pig are involved in activities for each of the seasons in this easy-to-read picture book.

Ehlert, Lois. *Color Zoo.* New York: J. B. Lippincott, 1989. (Caldecott Honor)
Zoo animals are produced by manipulating shapes and colors.

Gibbons, Gail. *Weather Forecasting.* Illustrated by the author. New York: Four Winds Press, 1987.
This brightly illustrated book tells about weather and forecasting during the four seasons.

Goennel, Heidi. *Seasons*. Illustrated by the author. Boston: Little, Brown, 1986.
  The text and beautifully designed paintings depict favorite activities for each season.

Keats, Ezra Jack. *The Snowy Day*. Illustrated by the author. New York: Viking, 1962.
  A young black boy delights in his first snowfall.

Lauture, Denize. *Father and Son*. Illustrated by Jonathan Green. New York: Putnam (Philomel), 1992.
  A father and son share special times.

Lindgren, Astrid. *The Tomten*. Illustrated by Harold Wiberg. New York: Coward, McCann & Geoghegan, 1968.
  This is a beautifully illustrated story about cold winter nights when everyone is asleep and the Tomten watches over them.

McCully, Emily Arnold. *First Snow*. Illustrated by the author. New York: Harper & Row, 1985.
  A mouse family loads the old red pickup with sleds and skates for a winter outing in this wordless picture book.

Mack, Gail. *Yesterday's Snowman*. Illustrated by Erik Blegvad. New York: Pantheon Books, 1979.
  A family makes a beautiful snowman, but because of rain, the next day it is gone.

Neitzel, Shirley. *The Jacket I Wear in the Snow*. Illustrated by Nancy Winslow Parker. New York: Greenwillow Books, 1989.
  This book names the clothes that are worn in the snow.

Parnell, Peter. *Winter Barn*. Illustrated by the author. New York: Macmillan, 1986.
  This informational book tells about all kinds of feathered, furry, scaly, and creepy creatures that come into the barn during the winter.

Ryder, Joanne. *White Bear, Ice Bear*. Illustrated by Michael Rothman. New York: Morrow Junior Books, 1989.
  A polar bear tells about his life and habits.

Stanley, Diane. *Moe the Dog in Tropical Paradise*. Illustrated by Elise Primavira. New York: G. P. Putman's Sons, 1992.
  Moe the dog and his friend Arlene cannot afford a tropical winter vacation, so they make their own at home.

Tresselt, Alvin. *White Snow, Bright Snow*. Illustrated by Roger Duvoisin. New York: Lothrop, Lee & Shepard, 1947. (Caldecott Medal)
  This book puts into words and pictures the excitement that snow brings to children.

Webster, Harriet. *Winter Book*. Illustrated by Irene Trivas. New York: Charles Scribner's Sons, 1988.
  This information book on wintertime activities contains outdoor games and nature studies as well as a chapter on celebrations.

Weiss, Nicki. *Dog Boy Cap Skate*. Illustrated by the author. New York: Greenwillow Books, 1989.
  This book's one-word expressions tell a story about a boy and girl ice skating.

Zeifeit, Harriet. *The Small Potatoes and the Snowball Fight*. Illustrated by Richard Brown. New York: Dell (Dell/Yearling Books/Small Potatoes Club Series), 1986.
A safety lesson is presented, along with ideas of things to do with snow.

Zolotow, Charlotte. *Something Is Going to Happen*. Illustrated by Catherine Stock. New York: Harper & Row, 1988.
A family finds that the first snowfall has happened.

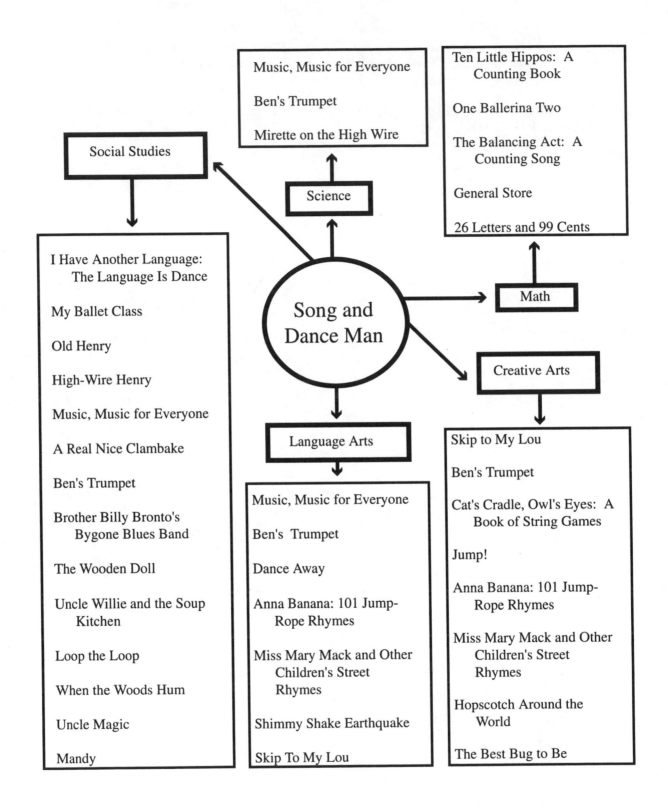

Music, Music for Everyone

Ben's Trumpet

Mirette on the High Wire

Ten Little Hippos: A Counting Book

One Ballerina Two

The Balancing Act: A Counting Song

General Store

26 Letters and 99 Cents

Social Studies

Science

Math

Song and Dance Man

Creative Arts

Language Arts

I Have Another Language: The Language Is Dance

My Ballet Class

Old Henry

High-Wire Henry

Music, Music for Everyone

A Real Nice Clambake

Ben's Trumpet

Brother Billy Bronto's Bygone Blues Band

The Wooden Doll

Uncle Willie and the Soup Kitchen

Loop the Loop

When the Woods Hum

Uncle Magic

Mandy

Music, Music for Everyone

Ben's Trumpet

Dance Away

Anna Banana: 101 Jump-Rope Rhymes

Miss Mary Mack and Other Children's Street Rhymes

Shimmy Shake Earthquake

Skip To My Lou

Skip to My Lou

Ben's Trumpet

Cat's Cradle, Owl's Eyes: A Book of String Games

Jump!

Anna Banana: 101 Jump-Rope Rhymes

Miss Mary Mack and Other Children's Street Rhymes

Hopscotch Around the World

The Best Bug to Be

7

Song and Dance Man

Ackerman, Karen. *Song and Dance Man.* Illustrated by Stephen Gammell. New York: Alfred A. Knopf, 1988. (Caldecott Medal)

Genre: Picture book

Summary: Grandpa shows some of the songs, dances, and jokes from the good old days when he was a song and dance man on the vaudeville stage.

Content Areas: Language arts, math, science, social studies, and creative arts. This book can be used to introduce a social studies unit on the impact of music on the lives of students or for a music unit on sounds.

Brainstorming Starters:

Tap shoes	Shammy cloth
Tap dancing	Piano player
Soft shoe	Vaudeville stage
Gliding	Spotlight
Cane	Jokes
Music	Good old days
Top hat	Grandfather
Twinkle	

Activities for Language Arts

"Song and Dance Pictures"

Ask students to look at the pictures in *Song and Dance Man*; *Music, Music for Everyone*; and *Ben's Trumpet* and think about what the three books have in common. Have the students write their responses in their journals. Ask volunteers to share their responses. Read the books to the class and discuss the theme and events in each book. Have the students verify their earlier responses about the common features of the three books.

Divide the class into small groups to find pictures of children playing musical instruments or dancing. Have groups share the pictures with the class by placing them on a display board. Students can select a picture and write a story about what is happening in the picture. Have several students share their stories with the class, and then place the stories under the pictures on the display board.

"Dancing and Musical Words"

Write words such as *ringing*, *dancing*, *prancing*, *gliding*, *skipping*, *tapping*, and *soft shoe* on the chalkboard. Ask students what the words have in common. After responses from the students, read *Dance Away*. Ask the students to name words or phrases in the story that described the steps in the rabbits' dance. Divide the class into groups. Have them look at and read *Anna Banana: 101 Jump-Rope Rhymes*; *Miss Mary Mack and Other Children's Street Rhymes*; *Shimmy Shake Earthquake*; *and Skip to My Lou* to find words or phrases that have musical sounds. After making a list of the words and phrases found, have each group share and compare its findings with the class. Have each group use additional words and phrases to write musical poems. The poems can be glued to construction paper and decorated, and then all of the poems can be compiled in a class booklet.

"Chant"

Ask students to share any chants, raps, jump-rope rhymes, or rhyming poems they know with the class. Divide the students into groups of five to read *Dance Away*, *Anna Banana*; *Miss Mary Mack*; and *Shimmy Shake Earthquake* and to identify words, phrases, or poems that might be chanted while bouncing a ball, clapping, juggling, jumping rope, or to rap. After selecting one poem, have groups practice clapping hands, jumping rope, or bouncing a ball while chanting. Have each group perform its chant for the class. Encourage students to listen for other chants to share with the class on another occasion.

Activities for Math

"Musical Counting Books"

Place ten small toy musical instruments before the class, remove one at a time, and have volunteers tell how many remain. After this, have ten students come to the front of the class. Give each student one instrument. Ask one student at a time to sit down and have the class tell how many remain standing until only one remains. Read *Ten Little Hippos*, *One Ballerina Two*, and *The Balancing Act: A Counting Song*. Have students identify the number of hippos on each page of *Ten Little Hippos* and the number of elephants on each page of *The Balancing Act*. Divide the class into groups to make counting books using pictures of musical instruments. Provide magazines, newspapers, art supplies, construction paper, scissors, and markers. Give each group two options for making its counting book: starting with one instrument and adding a new instrument to each page with the final page having ten instruments, or starting with ten instruments and ending with one. Students can find pictures in magazines or draw their own illustrations. Each page should be numbered; words can be written to go with the pictures. The counting books can be shared with the class or placed in the math center.

"General Store"

Show pictures of different kinds of stores and tell the class to listen as you read *General Store*. Ask students how the general store in the book differs from the stores in the pictures. After discussing a general store, tell students you are going to create a classroom general store to study counting money. Set aside a small area for the general store. Ask students to bring in empty food boxes, plastic fruits and vegetables, flower and vegetable seeds, small toy musical instruments, jump ropes, strings, and items of clothing. Secure any items that students do not contribute, and provide a toy cash register. Divide the class into two groups to prepare the store. One group can arrange the items on shelves and price the items, with no price tag over fifty cents, while the other group can make street signs and advertisements for items on sale. Share *26 Letters and 99 Cents;* review the value of coins before students operate the general store. Give each student a group of pennies, nickels, and dimes. Have students sort their coins and count the number of each denomination. Review how many pennies equal a nickel, how many pennies equal a dime, and how many nickels equal a dime. Hold up an item with a price tag. Ask the class to hold up the coins needed to buy the item. Continue this procedure until students understand. Divide into groups. Give each group cards bearing such questions as, "How many pennies would it take to buy something that costs seven cents?" or "If you have ten cents and buy a five-cent jump rope, how much will you get back?" Have each group answer the question cards and swap cards with other groups. As the students play store, have some group members serve as storekeepers while others are the customers. While one group goes to the general store, the other groups can develop newspaper ads by cutting out items from old magazines and newspapers. The selected items can be glued onto blank sheets of paper and the price written alongside. These can be placed in the math center for small group work. Give each small group an amount of money to spend for purchasing some of the advertised items. Groups decide how many purchases can be made with this money and then list their selections with prices. Display lists of selections in the math center.

Activities for Science

"Sounds"

Introduce a study of sounds by playing music that features various musical instruments and sounds. Ask students if the sounds are all the same or if they are different. Introduce the concept that sounds can be loud or soft and high or low. Using a primary-grade music triangle, demonstrate how to make loud and soft sounds by striking with more or less force. Make various sounds on a musical instrument, such as the triangle. Have students identify the sounds as loud or soft. Show how slow and fast vibrations result in low and high sounds.

Make a chart with the headings *stringed*, *wind*, and *percussion*. Tell students that musical instruments fall into one of these categories. Show pictures of various instruments, such as a guitar, flute, and drum, and have students place the pictures in the proper column on the chart. Ask students to identify any instruments not pictured and write the name of the instrument in the proper category. Divide the class into groups to identify additional musical instruments and to find or draw pictures of them. Have the students add their drawings to the proper column on the chart. Display the groups' findings and introduce the sounds made by the different instruments. If the school has a music or band teacher, invite the teacher to demonstrate instruments for the class and to guide the students as they make sounds on the instruments. If a music or band teacher is not available, demonstrate the various sounds on a piano, drum, horn, guitar, or other musical instrument. Allow the groups to try making sounds on the instruments.

After each group has had the opportunity to make sounds, ask students how we hear. After students generate ideas, show a model of the ear to show how sound enters the ear and passes through the canal to the nerve endings, which carry the message to the brain. Brainstorm to find out what students know about how the ear can be damaged by loud sounds and injuries. Clear up any concerns students might have about ears. Have them make a list of ways to protect their hearing. Display the lists.

"Musical Instruments"

Make tapping sounds by striking a table. Provide objects that make various sounds, such as glasses with different amounts of water, keys jingling, a spoon and pan, popping popcorn, and rubber bands strung across a box. Identify different objects that can be used to make music. Read *Music, Music for Everyone* and *Ben's Trumpet*. Ask students to identify the musical instruments in each book. Provide boxes, bottles, rubber bands, spoons, and other materials for students to make musical instruments. When the instruments have been made, allow students to play music on the instruments. Display the instruments on a table in front of a bulletin board.

"Gravity"

Place a balance beam in front of the class and allow students to walk on it. Discuss the difficulty of staying on the beam and ask students to identify other activities that require good balancing skills.

Ask a student to hold a ball, drop it, and throw it up into the air. Ask why the ball fell to the ground. Introduce the idea that gravity pulls things to the earth. Have the students jump and note that they always come down. Have them make paper airplanes and observe how the pull of gravity brings them back to the ground. Read *Mirette on the High Wire* and ask the students if there is a pull on a person walking on a high wire or climbing a ladder. Ask students why maintaining their center of gravity when dancing or performing on balance beams or tightropes is very important. Have them suggest what would happen if they lost their balance or proper form. Divide the class into groups to demonstrate the importance of balance in the pull of gravity. Have the students touch their toes to a wall and then try to stand on their toes. Have the students place their heels against the wall and then try to pick up a paper clip from the floor. Ask students why these activities are difficult. Have students sit on the floor, wrap their arms around their knees, and rock back and forth to music while raising and lowering their feet. Have the students discuss why balance during movements to music and why rhythm in performance are important. Have students practice (separately) walking on a balance beam and juggling. After practicing these activities, use the story starter, "The Day the Earth Lost All Gravity . . ." or "When I Lost My Balance . . ." to write a story. Encourage students to illustrate their stories for display on the bulletin board.

"Magnetism"

Question students to see what they know about magnetism. Clarify the concept of magnetism by demonstrating how magnets work and by showing pictures in which forces act on an object, such as magnets holding notes on a refrigerator door. Introduce the concept of magnetic poles by showing bar- or horseshoe-shaped magnets. Demonstrate attraction and repulsion. Use two horseshoe or bar magnets to point out that the earth has similar poles and explain how a compass with a magnetic needle can be used to find north. Give small groups of students a magnet and several objects including paper clips, coins, cookie sheets, cake pans, and nails. Ask students to determine whether the magnet attracts each of the objects. The findings of each group can be shared with the class. Have other groups of students observe the actions of compasses by first walking from one point to another in a straight line you have marked. Then have them follow a ten-foot square path you have marked. Ask the students to observe the compass as they follow the straight line and the square. The groups should be prepared to tell the class any differences they observed in the actions of the compass during the experiment.

Activities for Social Studies

"Dance Classes"

Send a note to parents of students who have taken dance classes, requesting pictures of students dressed in their costumes or videotapes of recitals. Display the pictures with pictures of other dancers, different types of dancing shoes, costumes, and other dance-related materials. Encourage brainstorming to find out what the students know about dance classes. Ask them to write questions they would like to know about dancing and write the questions on the chalkboard. Have them listen while you read *I Have Another Language: The Language Is Dance* and *My Ballet Class* for information that might answer the questions. Have the students answer the questions they posed earlier. Plan to have a dance instructor or another resource person visit the class to answer any questions that could not be answered by reading the books. Have the instructor and students demonstrate different kinds of dances and steps. Ask the dance instructor to plan a simple dance activity for the entire class. After the performance, allow students who brought costumes to class tell when they wore them. If students brought videos, show the part of the video that features the student. If there is a ballet performance, dance recital, or other performance in your area or on television, encourage students to attend or watch the performance. If possible, take the class to a dance performance or view the television performance together. Encourage students to bring to class newspaper or magazine pictures or stories about young dancers.

"Cooperation Counts"

Show pictures of different kinds of parades. Have students tell about parades they have attended. Encourage them to tell why there was a parade and then describe what they saw during the parade. Have the students look closely at the bands in the parade pictures and name the musical instruments. Through questions and suggestions, help students arrive at the conclusion that to give a good performance each member of the band must cooperate and that the entire band must spend a large amount of time practicing before performing. Read *Old Henry*; *High-Wire Henry*; *Music, Music for Everyone*; and *A Real Nice Clambake* to the class. Ask students to identify cooperative and uncooperative actions in these stories. Divide the class into groups. Each group may either write a new ending for one of the stories to show cooperative or uncooperative actions or may draw two pictures of a band in which members are uncooperative in the first picture and cooperative in the second. Have the groups share their products with the class and display them on a bulletin board under the heading *Cooperation Counts*.

"Traveling with a Band"

Share the books *Music, Music for Everyone* and *Ben's Trumpet*. Discuss the differences in how the children of the Oak Street Band in *Music, Music for Everyone* and Ben in *Ben's Trumpet* practiced their music. Ask students to explain how the stories' endings were similar and whether the stories might have been based on real events. After discussing the music of the Oak Street Band and Ben and the Zig Zag Club musicians, read *Brother Billy Bronto's Bygone Blues Band*. Ask students if the dinosaurs' band tour could have happened. After discussing the imaginary dinosaur band, tell the students you want them to plan a band tour. Divide the class into groups. Have each group select one of the three bands. Ask the groups to decide where the tour will go and what could happen. Have the groups work cooperatively to develop a story, write it or record it on tape, and draw pictures to illustrate it. Have each group share its story with the class.

"Each Can Share the Good Old Days"

Call attention to the sentence in *Song and Dance Man* that uses the term *the good old days* to describe the vaudeville shows. Ask students what the term means. Ask them to think about how long ago the good old days were; list their estimates on the board. After pointing out how the estimates vary, ask the students to describe what they think it was like in those days. Share *The Wooden Doll*, *Uncle Willie and the Soup Kitchen*, *Loop the Loop*, *When the Woods Hum*, *Uncle Magic*, and *Mandy* with the class. Have it discuss the events in the stories. Ask each student to consult another student to decide when the stories took place and if the events in the stories are like current situations in the community. Discuss and compare the students' opinions. Divide the class into pairs and ask them to estimate the ages of the characters in each story. After arriving at some consensus on the approximate ages of the characters, ask students to identify what the younger character learned from the older person in each story. Have the students share their ideas and discuss how each age group can learn from another. Ask the pairs of students to write a story that takes place forty years in the future, focusing on what they would tell a young character about the good old days when they were young. Have volunteers share their stories. Compile the stories and place them in the reading center.

Activities for Creative Arts

"Class Talent Show/Recital"

Ask students to select and read *Skip to My Lou*; *Ben's Trumpet*; *Cat's Cradle, Owl's Eyes: A Book of String Games*; *Jump!*; *Anna Banana*; *Miss Mary Mack*; *Hopscotch Around the World*, or *The Best Bug to Be*. Discuss and list the different talents and games described. Explain to the class what a talent show or recital is. Divide the class into groups to plan a talent show. Give students the option of singing, dancing, jumping rope, doing string design, doing magic tricks, playing instruments, or helping with scenery, props, and advertisements. Help the class set a time for the show. Have them make invitations for other classes and parents. After the show, have students write journal entries about it.

"Making Musical Instruments"

Have the class look at the use of silhouettes in *Ben's Trumpet* and discuss how you can make them. Demonstrate by drawing a silhouette of one student. Provide a light, black construction paper, a pencil, and scissors for students to make silhouettes of their musical instruments. Students can share their silhouettes with the class and place them on the bulletin board.

Bulletin Boards

"The Importance of Gravity"
In the center of the bulletin board place a magnetic strip and to it fasten the heading *The Importance of Gravity*, which is made from individual letters with magnetic tape on the back of each letter. Have the students place the pictures they drew to illustrate their stories written for the science activities "Gravity" and "Magnetism" on the bulletin board.

"We Make Music"
Cover the bulletin board with white paper. Place music notes cut from black construction paper around the edges of the board. Place the phrase *We Make Music* in the center of the bulletin board on a music staff drawn on construction paper. The students can place the silhouettes of musical instruments (from the creative arts activity "Making Musical Instruments") around the caption. Place musical instruments on a table in front of the bulletin board.

Related Books

Ackerman, Karen. *Song and Dance Man*. Illustrated by Stephen Gammell. New York: Alfred A. Knopf, 1988.
Grandpa shows some of the songs, dances, and jokes from the good old days when he was a song and dance man on the vaudeville stage.

Birchman, David F. *Brother Billy Bronto's Bygone Blues Band*. Illustrated by John O'Brien. New York: Lothrop, Lee & Shepard, 1992.
A dinosaur blues band from New Orleans goes on a tour in this book of rhyme and rhythm.

Blos, Joan W. *Old Henry*. Illustrated by Stephen Gammell. New York: William Morrow, 1987.
Henry is a nonconformist who moves into a settled neighborhood; both Henry and his neighbors realize that compromise may be necessary.

Bonners, Susan. *The Wooden Doll*. New York: Lothrop, Lee & Shepard, 1991.
A little girl learns the secret of her name and gets a special doll from her immigrant grandfather.

Booth, Barbara D. *Mandy*. Illustrated by Jim Lamarche. New York: Lothrop, Lee & Shepard, 1991.
A hearing-impaired girl braves a stormy night to help her grandmother find a lost pin.

Calhoun, Mary. *High-Wire Henry*. Illustrated by Erick Ingraham. New York: Morrow Junior Books, 1991.
Henry's jealousy of the new puppy does not stop him from helping the puppy when it gets into trouble.

Cole, Joanna, compiler. *Anna Banana: 101 Jump-Rope Rhymes*. Illustrated by Alan Tiegreen. New York: William Morrow, 1989.
This book contains 101 jump-rope rhymes.

Cole, Joanna, and Stephanie Calmenson. *Miss Mary Mack and Other Children's Street Rhymes*. Illustrated by Alan Tiegreen. New York: Morrow Junior Books, 1990.
This book contains a number of street rhymes for ball bouncing, counting out, and hand clapping.

DiSalvo-Ryan, DyAnne. *Uncle Willie and the Soup Kitchen*. New York: Morrow Junior Books, 1991.
Uncle Willie's example teaches his young nephew about compassion.

Dugan, Barbara. *Loop the Loop*. Illustrated by James Stevenson. New York: Greenwillow Books, 1992.
The bond of friendship between an old woman and a young girl is not dampened when the woman goes to a nursing home.

Field, Rachel. *General Store*. Illustrated by Nancy Winslow Parker, 1988. New York: Greenwillow Books, 1926.
A girl dreams of owning a store with merchandise from calico to garden seeds.

French, Vivian. *One Ballerina Two*. Illustrated by Jan Ormerod. New York: Lothrop, Lee & Shepard, 1991.
The colorful illustrations in this counting book feature two ballerinas.

Gauch, Patricia Lee. *Uncle Magic*. Illustrated by Deborah Kogan Ray. New York: Holiday House, 1992.
A little girl's uncle creates a time of magic.

Gryski, Camilla. *Cat's Cradle, Owl's Eyes: A Book of String Games*. Illustrated by Tom Sankey. New York: Beech Tree Books, 1983.
This book gives basic instructions for making string games.

Hammerstein, Oscar. *A Real Nice Clambake*. Music by Richard Rodgers. Illustrated by Nadine Bernard Westcott. Boston: Little, Brown (Joy Street Books), 1992.
A New England clambake offers good food and promotes friendship.

Hoban, Tana. *26 Letters and 99 Cents*. New York: Greenwillow Books, 1987.
This book contains color photographs of letters, numbers, and coins.

Isadora, Rachel. *Ben's Trumpet*. New York: Mulberry Books, 1979. (Caldecott Honor)
Ben plays an imaginary trumpet until he is discovered by musicians from the Zig Zag Club.

———. *My Ballet Class*. Illustrated by the author. New York: Greenwillow Books, 1980.
This picture book shows a ballet class.

Jabar, Cynthia. *Shimmy Shake Earthquake*. Boston: Little, Brown, 1992.
Eighteen dance poems appropriate for all age groups are included.

Johnson, Delores. *The Best Bug to Be*. Illustrated by the author. New York: Macmillan, 1992.
Though Kelly does not get the lead in the school play, she steals the show as the bumblebee.

Kalbfleisch, Susan. *Jump!* Illustrated by Laurie McGugan. New York: William Morrow, 1985.
    An instruction book that shows how to jump rope.

Lankford, Mary D. *Hopscotch Around the World.* Illustrated by Karen Milone. New York: Morrow Junior Books, 1992.
    This book gives directions for several varieties of hopscotch from around the world.

McCarthy, Bobette. *Ten Little Hippos: A Counting Book.* Illustrated by the author. New York: Bradbury Press, 1992.
    This counting book counts down from ten with little hippos in a Broadway revue.

McCully, Emily. *Mirette on the High Wire.* New York: Putnam, 1992.
    Mirette helps a fearful wire-walker return to the high wire.

Peek, Merle. *The Balancing Act: A Counting Song.* Illustrated by the author. New York: Clarion Books, 1987.
    In this counting song book the elephants perform a balancing act for their animal friends.

Ryder, Joanne. *When the Woods Hum.* Illustrated by Catherine Stock. New York: Morrow Junior Books, 1991.
    A beautiful family story in which the father explains the life cycle of cicadas to his daughter, who in turn explains it to her son.

Schick, Eleanor. *I Have Another Language: The Language Is Dance.* Illustrated by the author. New York: Macmillan, 1992.
    This picture book beautifully illustrates the excitement of a first dance recital.

Shannon, George. *Dance Away.* Illustrated by Jose Aruego and Ariane Dewey. New York: Mulberry Books, 1991.
    Rabbit uses his love of dancing to save his friends from a fox.

Westcott, Nadine Bernard. *Skip to My Lou.* Illustrated by the author. Boston: Little, Brown (Joy Street Books), 1989.
    When a boy's parents leave him in charge of the farm for a day, the animals humorously dance to the song "Skip to My Lou."

Williams, Vera. B. *Music, Music for Everyone.* New York: Mulberry Books, 1984.
    Rosa and her friends form the Oak Street Band to help pay the expenses of Rosa's grandmother's illness.

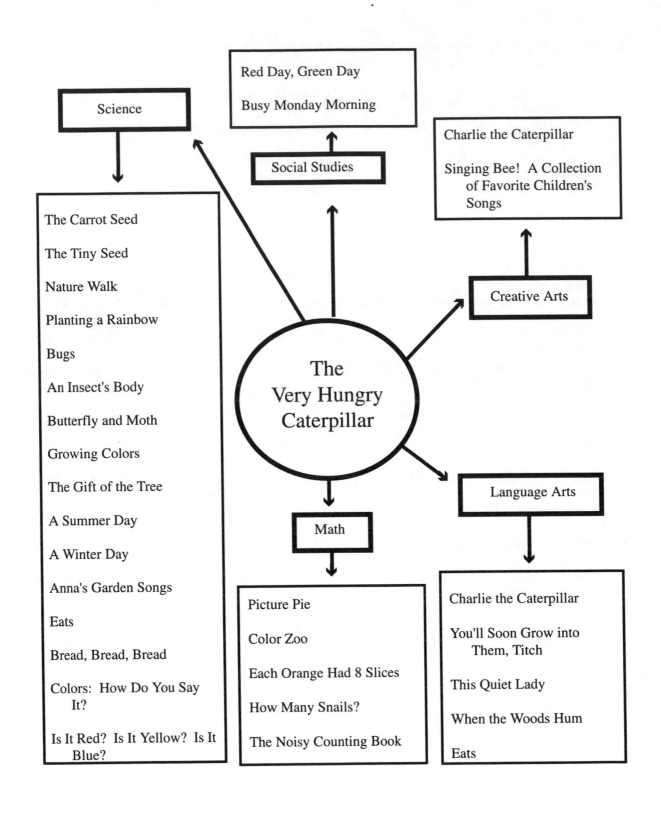

Science

The Carrot Seed

The Tiny Seed

Nature Walk

Planting a Rainbow

Bugs

An Insect's Body

Butterfly and Moth

Growing Colors

The Gift of the Tree

A Summer Day

A Winter Day

Anna's Garden Songs

Eats

Bread, Bread, Bread

Colors: How Do You Say It?

Is It Red? Is It Yellow? Is It Blue?

Red Day, Green Day

Busy Monday Morning

Social Studies

Charlie the Caterpillar

Singing Bee! A Collection of Favorite Children's Songs

Creative Arts

The Very Hungry Caterpillar

Language Arts

Math

Picture Pie

Color Zoo

Each Orange Had 8 Slices

How Many Snails?

The Noisy Counting Book

Charlie the Caterpillar

You'll Soon Grow into Them, Titch

This Quiet Lady

When the Woods Hum

Eats

8

The Very Hungry Caterpillar
द

Carle, Eric. *The Very Hungry Caterpillar*. New York: Philomel, 1987.

Genre: Counting book

Summary: A caterpillar appears to eat holes in the pages of this book as it eats a variety of food and builds a cocoon. After two weeks, the caterpillar emerges as a beautiful butterfly.

Content Areas: Language arts, math, science, social studies, and creative arts. This book can be used to introduce units on days of the week, counting from one to five, transformation of caterpillars, nutrition, or colors.

Brainstorming Starters:

Caterpillar	Thursday
Cocoon	Friday
Butterfly	Saturday
Small	Hungry
Big	Ate through
Fat	Stomachache
Leaf	Food
Green	Fruit
Days of the week	Apple
Monday	Pear
Tuesday	Strawberry
Wednesday	Orange

Activities for Language Arts

"Mural Story Map"

After reading *The Very Hungry Caterpillar* and *Charlie the Caterpillar*, divide the class by pairing students. Have them list things that the caterpillars ate and retell the story in sequence by recalling what was eaten each day of the week. Allow students who are having difficulty remembering the sequence to consult other students. A mural story map for *The Very Hungry Caterpillar* can be made by dividing the class into groups by days of the week. Have each group draw a picture to represent what the caterpillar ate on that day. Place the pictures in sequence on a six-foot-long section of butcher paper. Display the mural as related books are read.

"Changes"

Have students examine the books *You'll Soon Grow into Them, Titch*; *This Quiet Lady*; and *When the Woods Hum.* Ask students to tell how they have changed since they were babies. After students make individual lists of changes, have small groups of students compare their lists and project future changes in their lives. Based on the projections, have students create individual stories beginning "When I grow up. . . ." Encourage students to illustrate their stories and share them with classmates. Ask each student to bring in a baby picture and a current school picture. Pair pictures on the bulletin board with the student's illustrated story.

"Creating a Class Story"

Read aloud *Eats.* Ask the class, "What do you think caterpillars eat?" Tell the class that new stories will be created after groups decide on new things for the caterpillar to eat. Divide the class into groups and assign each group a letter. Have the groups select one junk food and one nutritious food beginning with the assigned letter. For example, a group assigned the letter *C* might choose cookies and carrots. Then the group must decide whether the new story should be about nutritious food, junk food, or both. Have groups share their stories with the class. When all stories have been shared, identify similarities and differences among the stories.

Activities for Math

"Shapes"

Share the book *Picture Pie* with the class. Display a large poster board on which are drawn a circle, square, triangle, and rectangle. Display concrete objects for each of the shapes, for example, a ball, sandwich, arrowhead, and toy-size trailer from a tractor-trailer rig. Give each student a set of shapes cut from construction paper. Point to a shape on the large poster and have students hold up the same shape from their set. Divide the class into small groups. Have group members compare and match each shape from their sets of shapes.

Give each group approximately fifty pipe cleaners. The four shapes can be made by bending the pipe cleaners. Completed shapes can be glued to construction paper. Display the completed shapes (see page 69). Use the extra pipe cleaners to make animals, using one or more of the four shapes.

"Shaped Counting Books"

After reading *Color Zoo, Each Orange Had 8 Slices, How Many Snails?*, and *The Noisy Counting Book,* divide the class into eight groups for making shaped counting books. Give each student five sheets cut in one shape: circle, triangle, square, or rectangle. Give students the option of finding pictures that match the assigned shape or drawing pictures in the assigned shape. There should be one object on the first page, two on the second, and so on. Have students write the corresponding number on the top or bottom of each page. Staple the pages together and share with other groups.

"Sorting by Color and Number"

Place five open boxes on a table. Color each box and tape a number on the front. In each box place number cards bearing the numbers one through five, colored cards of five different colors, and counting cards with one to five objects pictured on each card. Pairs of students go to the table and

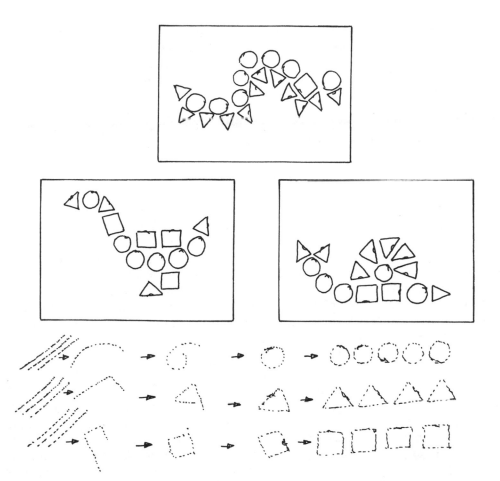

sort the cards by counting the objects, identifying the number, or sorting by color. One student in the pair sorts while the other checks the sorted cards. When all students have had the opportunity to sort the cards, discuss why it is important to know how to identify and sort numbers or objects.

Activities for Science

"From Seeds to Plants"

Plan a field trip to an orchard, market, nursery, or farm to discover the sources of fruits, vegetables, and trees. Before going on the field trip, read *The Carrot Seed*, *The Tiny Seed*, *Nature Walk*, and *Planting a Rainbow*. Discuss what to look for and questions to ask while on the field trip. After returning from the field trip, review the questions and record what was learned on a chart. Review the books that were read before the field trip.

Have the students walk around the school grounds to collect different leaves. Display the leaves and use a magnifying glass to look at them. Ask students to point out any differences, such as colors or sizes, in the leaves. Sentences dictated by the students about the leaves can be written on a chart. Make a collage of leaves that were collected and display the collage with the chart.

Group students and give each group a plastic bag that contains several kinds of large seeds (i.e., pumpkin or sunflower) and several small cards. Have students sort the seeds and tape seeds that are alike or very similar on the cards. For example, one card may have large seeds, another black seeds of all sizes. After sorting the seeds, have groups describe the classification system(s) they used. On the chalkboard list the names of any seeds that students can identify. Have students locate pictures of the plants that grow from these seeds. Make a display by matching the seeds with the plant pictures. Plant two or three seeds in small plastic cups. Allow students to check the growth of their plant each day. Have students fold a sheet of paper so that it forms an accordion-like booklet. Students can use the booklet by recording their daily observations on succeeding sections. The observations may be in words or in pictures with a word about each picture. After the accordion booklet has been filled, allow the student to take the booklet and plant home.

"Baby or Adult"

Share the books *Bugs, An Insect's Body, Butterfly and Moth,* and *The Gift of the Tree* with the class. Display pictures of insects in various stages of growth. Help students identify these stages as you call attention to each picture. Provide magazines and have students cut out pictures of insects. The pictures can be glued on poster board and labeled *Baby, Young,* and *Adult,* or the pictures can be grouped by gluing an adult and baby of like species on one sheet and writing the name of the species below. Have students write a story about the life of one of these insects. Following this activity, have students collect small pictures of baby and adult insects and paste them on small cards. Divide the class into groups. Have students in one group swap cards with another group and sequence the cards to show the life cycle of the pictured insects.

"Seasons"

Review seasons of the year by reading *Colors: How Do You Say It?; Is It Red? Is It Yellow? Is It Blue?; Growing Colors, A Summer Day;* and *A Winter Day.* Display pictures that contain scenes that characterize various seasons. Have the students describe the pictures. Ask students to fold a sheet of paper into four equal parts and label each with a different season. Write each of the four seasons in four columns on the board. Challenge students to think of words that describe each season and write them in the appropriate section on their paper. Ask students to share their lists. Write their suggestions on the board under the appropriate heading. Discuss the lists and add additional characteristics.

Divide the class into groups to make seasonal collages. Give each group four paper plates and magazines. Label each paper plate with a different season. Have students cut out pictures of seasons and glue them on the appropriate plates. Have students share their finished collages with the class and display them on a bulletin board.

"Nutritious and Junk Food"

Read *Anna's Garden Songs; Eats;* and *Bread, Bread, Bread.* Discuss favorite foods of class members and list them on the board. Make a chart showing the most popular and least popular foods. Introduce the four food groups by having a poster-board chart that has four sections, each a different color, to represent the four food groups—meat, grain, dairy, and fruits and vegetables. Ask students why we need food from each group and why we need different amounts of food from each group throughout our lives. Have students collect pictures of food from magazines and newspapers. Be sure they collect at least one picture to represent each food group. Have the students mount their pictures on sheets of construction paper that match the colors used for the food groups on the chart. Call out the name of a food group and have students hold up pictures of foods in that group, such as cheese for the dairy group. Have students fold a piece of paper in fourths. Have students unfold the paper and outline the sections in the color assigned to the food groups. Then have students draw or glue a picture of an appropriate food in each section.

Discuss foods that are not healthy, such as candy, cakes, and soft drinks. Place pictures of junk food or healthy foods not commonly eaten by children (i.e., broccoli) in a paper grab bag. Divide the class into pairs, and have each student select an item from the grab bag. Ask students to use their selection to role-play refusing junk foods or tasting an unfamiliar healthy food. Suggest nutritious alternatives to junk food and allow students to identify healthy foods by collecting pictures from magazines and newspapers.

Ask volunteers to discuss planning nutritious meals. Divide the class into cooperative groups. Give each group a blank sheet of paper (on which to write the menu) and two paper place mats (one for healthy foods on one for junk foods). Have the students glue appropriate foods on the place mats. Display the menus on the bulletin board and the place mats on a display board. Discuss the consequences of eating good foods and junk foods; list the students' ideas on the chalkboard. Following the discussion, have students draw and label that illustrate the consequences of various eating habits. For example, a picture of a tired student might bear the caption "Joe eats junk food," while a picture of an active student might bear the caption "Fred eats food from the four food groups." Have students share their pictures. Conclude the study by developing a mural of foods labeled according to nutritional value or food group, such as, "junk food," dairy product," "meat," and so forth.

Activities for Social Studies

"Calendar"

Read *Red Day, Green Day* and *Busy Monday Morning*. Show the class a large calendar for the present month. Discuss the different parts of the calendar. Write numbers and days of the week on large cards. Mix up the cards and hold them up one at a time, having students volunteer to point out on the calendar the day of the week or the date indicated on the card. Ask for volunteers to find the first day of the month and any special days that are marked on the calendar. Give each student a blank calendar, a set of seven cards with the days of the week, and a set of cards with the numbers one through ten. Using the cards as a guide, have the students fill in the blank calendar with the days of the week and the dates of the first ten days. When all students can complete this activity, distribute another blank calendar. Hold up day and number cards in random order and have students write the day or number in the correct blank spaces on their calendar.

Ask students to name foods eaten by the caterpillar. List the foods on the board. Have students write the name of one food on each of the first ten days of their calendar. Display the calendars or allow students to take them home.

Brainstorm activities that occur on different days of the week. List all suggested ideas on the board, and then classify the activities by the appropriate day of the week. Have students think about which day is their favorite day of the week. Allow volunteers to identify their favorite day and tell why they like it best. Have students draw a picture or write a story about their favorite day of the week.

"My Street"

After reading *The Very Hungry Caterpillar*, ask students to recall and list the different foods eaten by the caterpillar. Ask students if all of these foods can be found in their neighborhood. Ask students to think of foods that might be found in their neighborhood that are not included in the story. Students may answer by drawing pictures and labeling them in response to the question "What could a caterpillar eat on my street?" Place the pictures on a display board. Working in small groups, have students research foods found in another part of the country or world. After making a list of these foods, have them respond to the story starter "What a caterpillar could eat in. . ." by writing and illustrating a cooperative story. Bring the class together to share the stories and identify foods common to all or most groups.

Activities for Creative Arts

"Pattern Necklaces"

Display a sample necklace made of pieces of drinking straw and beads. Provide a large supply of colored beads, plastic drinking straws cut into one-inch lengths, and thirty pieces of ribbon cut in 2-inch lengths. Have students string beads and straws to create color patterns. Tie the ends of the ribbon and allow students to wear the necklaces.

"Fluttering"

After reading *The Very Hungry Caterpillar* and *Charlie the Caterpillar*, tell students they can pretend to be a caterpillar by stretching, curling, and turning into a butterfly and fluttering. Ask for volunteers to lead the class as they stretch, curl, and flutter. Change leaders several times; encourage them to try a variety of movements.

"Mobile"

Provide art supplies for making a mobile and divide the class into groups. Have students create mobiles that represent the transformation from caterpillar to butterfly. Display the completed mobiles in the classroom.

"Songs"

Familiarize students with songs from *Singing Bee! A Collection of Favorite Children's Songs.* Sing songs from the collection and make up songs about butterflies, animals, days of the week, and colors.

Bulletin Boards

"Butterflies"

Have students make the background of the bulletin board by painting a blue sky with colorful flowers glued to the bottom portion of the board. Place a cloud made from cotton balls with a large, colorful caterpillar below it, in the center of the board. Have students design a butterfly from pipe cleaners, tissue paper, and construction paper. Also have them write a sentence about the butterfly. Attach each butterfly and its accompanying sentence to the bulletin board with pushpins.

"Caterpillar Words"

Have students make the background for the bulletin board by drawing a branch of a tree with leaves on it. Give each student a caterpillar made from brown construction paper. Have the students write a word about caterpillars (i.e., little, fuzzy, or hungry) on each caterpillar, with one letter in each segment of the caterpillar. These caterpillar words can be placed on the bulletin board under the heading *Caterpillar Words*.

Related Books

Adoff, Arnold. *Eats*. Illustrated by Susan Russo. New York: Lothrop, Lee & Shepard, 1979.
    This book of poetry celebrates food.

Carle, Eric. *The Tiny Seed*. Saxonville, Mass.: Picture Book Studio, 1987.
    This story shows the growth of a flower from a seed.

———. *The Very Hungry Caterpillar*. New York: Philomel, 1987.
    A caterpillar appears to eat holes in the pages of this book as it eats a variety of food and builds a cocoon. After two weeks, the caterpillar emerges as a beautiful butterfly.

Cole, Joanna. *An Insect's Body*. Photographs by Jerome Wexler and Raymond Mendez. New York: William Morrow, 1984.
    Photographs are used to show the insect's body.

Deluise, Dom. *Charlie the Caterpillar*. Illustrated by Christopher Santoro. New York: Simon & Schuster, 1990.
    No one will play with Charlie until he is transformed from an ugly caterpillar into a beautiful butterfly.

Domanska, Janina. *Busy Monday Morning*. Illustrated by the author. New York: Greenwillow Books, 1985.
    The days of the week are taught through a Polish folk song.

Dunham, Meredith. *Colors: How Do You Say It?* New York: Lothrop, Lee & Shepard, 1987.
   This book gives the names of colors in four languages: English, French, Italian, and Spanish.

Ehlert, Lois. *Color Zoo.* New York: J. B. Lippincott, 1989. (Caldecott Honor)
   Zoo animals are produced by manipulating colors and shapes.

————. *Planting a Rainbow.* Illustrated by the author. New York: Harcourt Brace Jovanovich, 1988.
   The bright illustrations show colors, seeds, and plants and tell how plants grow.

Emberley, Ed. *Picture Pie.* Boston: Little, Brown, 1984.
   Create pictures using the four basic shapes—circle, square, rectangle, and triangle.

Florian, Douglas. *Nature Walk.* New York: Greenwillow Books, 1989.
   This book introduces readers to the many highlights of nature on a walk through the woods.

————. *A Summer Day.* New York: Greenwillow Books, 1988.
   The book describes the events of a summer day for very young children.

————. *A Winter Day.* New York: Greenwillow Books, 1987.
   Illustrations describe a winter day.

Giganti, Paul, Jr. *Each Orange Had Eight Slices: A Counting Book.* Illustrated by Donald Crews. New York: Greenwillow Books, 1992.
   The words and illustrations in this counting book will interest beginning readers.

————. *How Many Snails?* Illustrated by Donald Crews. New York: Greenwillow Books, 1988.
   This counting book teaches the concept of division by subdividing a whole into subgroups.

Hart, Jane, ed. *Singing Bee! A Collection of Favorite Children's Songs.* Illustrated by Anita Lobel. New York: Lothrop, Lee & Shepard, 1982.
   One hundred twenty-five traditional songs and nursery rhymes are included in this collection.

Hoban, Tana. *Is It Red? Is It Yellow? Is It Blue?* New York: Mulberry Books, 1978.
   Colors, shapes, quantities, and directions are introduced.

Hutchins, Pat. *You'll Soon Grow into Them, Titch.* New York: Greenwillow Books, 1983.
   Titch adjusts to the problems of hand-me-down clothes that are too large.

Krauss, Ruth. *The Carrot Seed.* Illustrated by Crockett Johnson. New York: Harper & Row, 1945.
   After planting a carrot seed, a little boy waits for it to grow.

Kunhardt, Edith. *Red Day, Green Day.* Illustrated by Marylin Hafner. New York: Greenwillow Books, 1992.
   A kindergarten class adopts a different color for each day of the week.

McMillan, Bruce. *Growing Colors.* New York: Lothrop, Lee & Shepard, 1988.
   Photographs of orchards and gardens display color as they grow in nature.

Morris, Ann. *Bread, Bread, Bread.* Photographs by Ken Heyman. New York: Lothrop, Lee & Shepard, 1989.
   This book is a celebration of the many types of breads.

Parker, Nancy Winslow, and Joan Richards Wright. *Bugs*. Illustrated by Nancy Winslow Parker. New York: Greenwillow Books, 1987.
In a very humorous way, this book describes the physical characteristics, habits, and natural environment of a variety of common insects.

Ryder, Joanne. *When the Woods Hum*. Illustrated by Catherine Stock. New York: Morrow Junior Books, 1991.
A beautiful family story in which the father explains the life cycle of cicadas to his daughter, who in turn explains it to her son.

Schade, Susan. *The Noisy Counting Book*. Illustrated by Jon Buller. New York: Random House, 1987.
This cumulative story repeats animal sounds and counting from one to six.

Steele, Mary Q. *Anna's Garden Songs*. Illustrated by Lena Anderson. New York: Greenwillow Books, 1989.
Watercolors illustrate poems about fruits and vegetables.

Tresselt, Alvin. *The Gift of the Tree*. Illustrated by Henri Sorensen. New York: Lothrop, Lee & Shepard, 1972.
This beautifully illustrated book depicts the role of an oak tree in the nature cycle.

Whalley, Paul. *Butterfly and Moth*. Photographs by Colin Keates, Dave King, and Kim Taylor. New York: Alfred A. Knopf, 1988.
This book shows the life cycle of butterflies from egg to adult.

Zolotow, Charlotte. *This Quiet Lady*. Illustrated by Anita Lobel. New York: Greenwillow Books, 1992.
A child learns about her mother's early life by looking at her old pictures.

Folklore

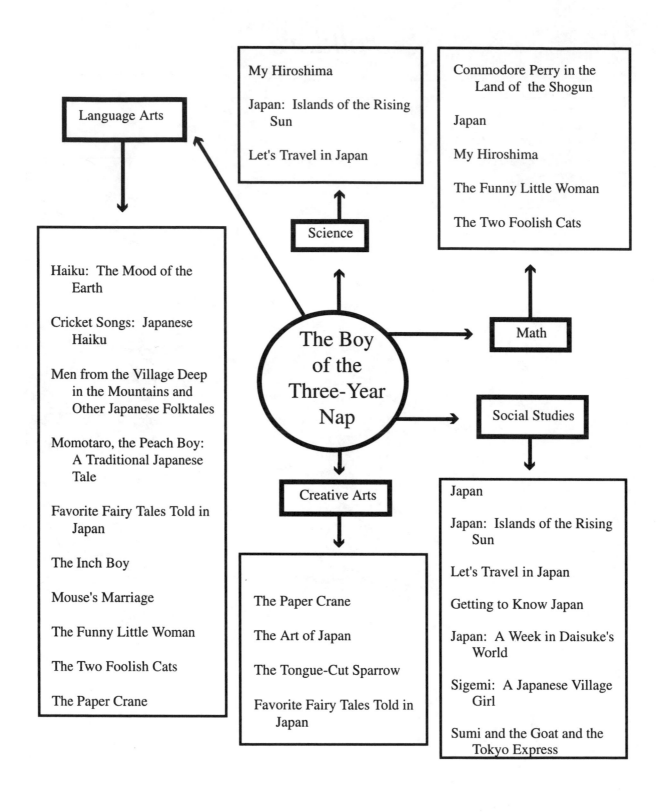

Language Arts

Haiku: The Mood of the Earth

Cricket Songs: Japanese Haiku

Men from the Village Deep in the Mountains and Other Japanese Folktales

Momotaro, the Peach Boy: A Traditional Japanese Tale

Favorite Fairy Tales Told in Japan

The Inch Boy

Mouse's Marriage

The Funny Little Woman

The Two Foolish Cats

The Paper Crane

My Hiroshima

Japan: Islands of the Rising Sun

Let's Travel in Japan

Commodore Perry in the Land of the Shogun

Japan

My Hiroshima

The Funny Little Woman

The Two Foolish Cats

Science

Math

Social Studies

The Boy of the Three-Year Nap

Creative Arts

The Paper Crane

The Art of Japan

The Tongue-Cut Sparrow

Favorite Fairy Tales Told in Japan

Japan

Japan: Islands of the Rising Sun

Let's Travel in Japan

Getting to Know Japan

Japan: A Week in Daisuke's World

Sigemi: A Japanese Village Girl

Sumi and the Goat and the Tokyo Express

9

The Boy of the Three-Year Nap

ॐ

Snyder, Dianne. *The Boy of the Three-Year Nap.* Illustrated by Allen Say. Boston: Houghton Mifflin, 1988. (Caldecott Honor, ALA Notable Children's Book)

Genre: Folktale

Summary: In this adaptation of a Japanese trickster tale, lazy Taro wins a wife and riches through a clever ruse.

Content Areas: Language arts, math, science, social studies, and creative arts. This book can be used to introduce a social studies unit on Japan.

Brainstorming Starters:

Kimono	Teahouse
Samurai	Tea ceremony
Island life	Origami
Location of Japan	Haiku
Japanese gods	Golden carp fish
Japanese gardens	Cormorants bird
Japanese customs	Ujigami patron god

Activities for Language Arts

"Haiku"

Share several haiku with the class from *Haiku: The Mood of the Earth* and *Cricket Songs: Japanese Haiku*. Prepare a pattern, following the sample below, to show the number of syllables on each line of a haiku.

5 syllables _ _ _ _ _
7 syllables _ _ _ _ _ _ _
5 syllables _ _ _ _ _

Have small groups of students use the pattern as a guide to create several poems and write them on the chalkboard. Read Japanese folktales such as *The Inch Boy* or *Mouse's Marriage* to the class and lead it on a silent walk outside, observing nature and listening to sounds. On returning to the classroom, have the students write additional haiku. Compile their poems into a booklet. Place the booklet on the reading table with other books of poetry.

"Sharing Japanese Folktales"

After reading *The Boy of the Three-Year Nap*; *Men from the Village Deep in the Mountains and Other Japanese Folktales*; *Momotaro, the Peach Boy: A Traditional Japanese Tale*; *Favorite Fairy Tales Told in Japan*; *The Funny Little Woman*; *The Two Foolish Cats*; and *The Paper Crane*, allow selected students to choose one of the books to read with an adult. After all of the books on the table have been read, have those students put on a literary circle for the entire class. Students can make invitations for the "Japanese Folktale Sharing Circle" and give them to the adult with whom they shared their book. Each student sharing a folktale may dress in a kimono and hat. After completing the sharing time, the books would be placed back on the reading table.

Activities for Math

"Compare the Time"

After sharing *Commodore Perry in the Land of the Shogun*, *Japan*, and *My Hiroshima*, display a map of Japan, a globe, and several clocks that show the time in various time zones. Display a map with each time zone shown in a different color. United States maps with time zones appear in many local white pages telephone books; for world maps with time zones, consult an encyclopedia under *Time*. Show the time in Tokyo on one manipulative clock and the local time on another clock. Give each student a small clock with movable hands. Have students suggest a time and have all students move the hands on their clock to that time. Students may check their work by comparing their clock to a clock that you hold. After changing the time several times, have students continue the project in pairs or in small groups.

Divide students into pairs. Provide each pair with two paper plates, markers, glue, hands for the clock faces, and a card marked with a time in the local time zone and in Japan. Have each pair make two clock faces showing the times written on the card. Remind students to point the short hand to the hour and the long hand to the minute. On the back of each clock, have students identify whether the time is in Japan or in United States.

"Rice Fractions"

After reading *The Funny Little Woman* and *The Two Foolish Cats*, introduce the words *divide*, *piece*, *largest*, *smallest*, *half*, and *whole*. Brainstorm to find out what students know about these words. Use pictures and a rice cake to demonstrate any concepts that are misunderstood. Divide the whole class into two groups to demonstrate half and halves. Then divide the class into pairs. Give one rice cake to each pair and instruct the students to divide the rice cakes into two parts. Have them compare the two parts to determine which is the largest.

Have each student find a picture of food in a magazine, cut it out, and glue it onto a round piece of construction paper, then cut their picture in half. Form groups of four or five students. Have each student give one half of each picture to another student in the group and place the other half in a pile in the center of the group. Each student must search through the pile to find the missing half, then glue both halves onto a piece of construction paper. Display the finished pictures in the classroom.

Activities for Science

"Islands"

Write the word *Island* on the chalkboard before reading *Japan: Islands of the Rising Sun*, *My Hiroshima*, and *Let's Travel in Japan*. Have students define the word, name any nearby islands, and tell what they know about islands. Divide the class into groups to research islands. Have one group find out how islands are formed or what makes them different from other land formations. This group can draw a picture to explain. Have another group study maps, globes, and other resources to find the names and sizes of large island countries. This information can be placed on a chart to show the class. Have a third group find pictures of various islands to share with the class. Have the group select one of the pictures and write about what it would be like to live on that island. Assign the fourth group the island of Japan. This group will find the country's location, size, how many large islands are in the group, the kind of land formations it has (i.e., mountains), and the name of the tallest mountain. This group can use pictures and charts for its report. Have each group share its research report with the class. After the reports have been given, point out Japan on a world map or globe and read *Japan: Islands of the Rising Sun* and *Let's Travel in Japan*. Ask students to name the bodies of water that would have to be crossed to get to Japan and also name the country closest to Japan. List the bodies of water and neighboring countries on the board. Ask each research group to plan an imaginary trip to Japan. Provide brochures and information books on Japan for this project. Have the groups decide whether to travel by airplane or boat and describe what the land looks like when they arrive. Each group can find or draw pictures of Japan or make a map to show the route it traveled from the United States to Japan. Have the groups share their report with the class; display the reports on the board.

Activities for Social Studies

"Mini-Textbook"

Gather resources on Japan, such as travel brochures, postcards, magazines, and information books. Have students bring additional information to class, if they can find it. Display these resources. After reading *The Boy of the Three-Year Nap*; *Japan*; *Japan: Islands of the Rising Sun*; *Let's Travel in Japan*; *Sigemi: A Japanese Village Girl*; *Sumi and the Goat and the Tokyo Express*; or *Getting to Know Japan*, have students prepare mini-textbooks by collecting pictures showing symbols, people, facts about, and places in Japan. Suggest separate pages be used for people, land, natural resources, transportation, food, products, traditions, and clothing. Each page should have a sentence to explain its content. Facts about Japan can be included on each page. A title page and a table of contents should be included. Completed books can be displayed on the bulletin board titled *Our Class Studies Japan*.

"Japanese Tea Ceremony"

After reading *Japan: A Week in Daisuke's World*, *Getting to Know Japan*, and *Let's Travel in Japan*, ask a teacher, parent, or someone from the community who is familiar with Japan to help the class learn about Japanese traditions, tea ceremonies, and meals. Plan a special event, such as a tea party, for the resource person's visit to the class. For this event, provide tea, five tea services, food, mats, and five small tables. Remind students to remove their shoes when they come to one of the five areas of the classroom that has been set up with a small table and four or five mats. Encourage students to wear traditional Japanese clothing during the special activity. After the party, discuss how a tea party in Japan is different from a similar party in our country. Students can ask the resource person to explain any concepts that are still unclear. The resource person should explain that the traditional dress and tea ceremony are just that—traditions, but that Japanese people usually wear modern clothing and often drink tea without the ritual.

Activities for Creative Arts

"Japanese Folktale Mobile"

After sharing *The Tongue-Cut Sparrow* or several Japanese folktales from *Favorite Fairy Tales Told in Japan*, have students select one to illustrate by making a mobile. Allowing those selecting the same folktale to work together. Provide art supplies for making the mobile, including two wire coat hangers for each mobile, string or wire to tie the hangers together, and art supplies to make the mobile figures. Have each group design and create one mobile, with each student completing a specific part of it. Completed mobiles can be displayed in the classroom.

"Designing Kimonos or Origami"

After reading *The Paper Crane* and *The Art of Japan*, provide art materials for making a paper kimono (see page 83). If an art teacher or a resource person is available, ask for help with this project. Have students make a small kimono. Provide a basic pattern made from butcher paper and a four-foot piece of uncut butcher paper. To make the kimono, tape the pattern pieces onto the butcher paper, cut out the pieces (cutting through the tape), staple or stitch the pieces together, and decorate with paint, fabric, and thread. Finished kimonos can be displayed in the room.

Bulletin Boards

"My State and Japan"
Using tagboard, cut out a fairly large map of your state. On another tagboard, cut out a map of Japan. Use pushpins to identify major cities and geographical features of each. Have students place facts they have learned around the map.

"Our Class Studies Japan"
Cut out an outline of Japan from construction paper. Write the phrase *Our Class Studies Japan* on it. Place the map in the center of the bulletin board. Have students place their mini-textbooks of Japan from the social studies activity "Mini-Textbook" around the map.

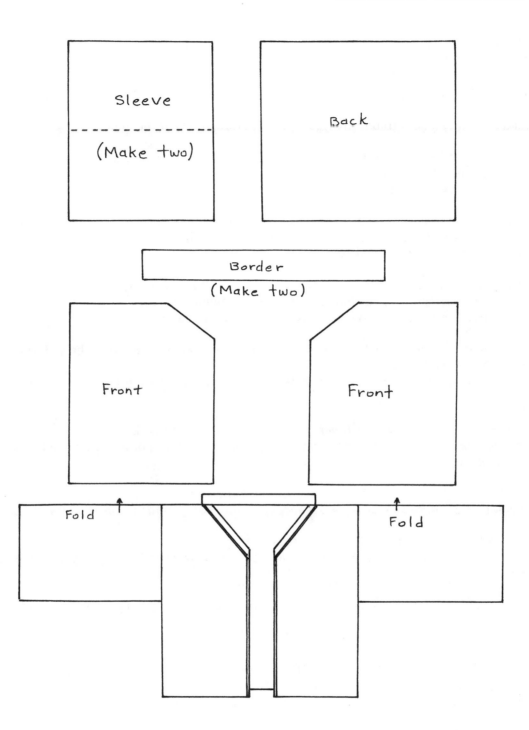

Related Books

Atwood, Ann. *Haiku: The Mood of the Earth*. Illustrated by the author. New York: Charles Scribner's
Sons, 1971.
Beautiful color photographs provide visual interpretations of the poems.

Bang, Garrett. *Men from the Village Deep in the Mountains and Other Japanese Folktales*. Illustrated
by the author. New York: Macmillan, 1973.
This is a collection of twelve Japanese folktales.

Bang, Molly. *The Paper Crane*. New York: Greenwillow Books, 1985.
This is a folktale about a man who pays for his dinner with a magical paper crane. It is beautifully
illustrated with three-dimensional collages.

Behn, Harry, translator. *Cricket Songs: Japanese Haiku*. Illustrations by Sesshu and other Japanese
masters. San Diego, Calif.: Harcourt Brace Jovanovich, 1964.
This collection of haiku about seasons is beautifully illustrated.

Blumberg, Rhoda. *Commodore Perry in the Land of the Shogun*. New York: Lothrop, Lee & Shepard,
1985. (Newbery Honor)
This information book examines Matthew Perry's role in opening Japan to world trade in the
1850s.

Geis, Darlene, ed. *Let's Travel in Japan*. Chicago: Children's Press, 1965.
An informational book that tells about the gardens, food, important dates, and other general
information on Japan.

Glubok, Shirley. *The Art of Japan*. New York: Macmillan, 1970.
This information book shows the Japanese love of beauty in the arts and crafts of Japan.

Greene, Carol. *Japan*. Chicago: Children's Press, 1983.
Some of Japan's geography, history, scenic treasures, culture, industry, and people are described
in this book.

Haviland, Virginia, ed. *Favorite Fairy Tales Told in Japan*. Illustrated by George Suyeoka. Boston:
Little, Brown, 1967.
This is an excellent collection of tales about animals and people.

Ishii, Momoko. *The Tongue-Cut Sparrow*. Translated by Katherine Paterson. Illustrated by Suekichi
Akaba. New York: E. P. Dutton (Lodestar Books), 1987.
This is a Japanese folktale of an old man and his greedy wife.

Jakeman, Alan. *Getting to Know Japan*. Illustrated by Don Lambo. New York: Coward, McCann &
Geoghegan, 1971.
This easy-to-read information book introduces Japan and its culture.

Kirk, Ruth. *Sigemi: A Japanese Village Girl*. Photographs by Ira Spring. New York: Harcourt, Brace
& World, 1965.
A pictorial story of family life, school and play, and religion and festivals in Japan.

Morimoto, Junko. *The Inch Boy*. Illustrated by the author. New York: Viking Kestrel, 1986.
A one-inch-tall boy sets sail in a rice-bowl boat, dreaming of becoming a famous samurai serving a noble lord.

———. *Mouse's Marriage*. Illustrated by the author. New York: Viking Kestral, 1986.
A Japanese folktale tells of a couple's search to find the mightiest husband in the world for their only daughter.

———. *My Hiroshima*. Illustrated by the author. New York: Viking Kestral, 1990.
Through illustrations, photographs, and collage, the author tells of her childhood in Hiroshima.

Mosel, Arlene. *The Funny Little Woman*. Illustrated by Blair Lent. New York: E. P. Dutton, 1972.
A rice dumpling rolled under the earth into the land of the wicked Oni who captures the funny little Japanese woman who chases after it.

Snyder, Dianne. *The Boy of the Three-Year Nap*. Illustrated by Allen Say. Boston: Houghton Mifflin, 1988.
In this adaptation of a Japanese trickster tale, lazy Taro wins a wife and riches through a clever ruse.

Shute, Linda. *Momotaro, the Peach Boy: A Traditional Japanese Tale*. Illustrated by the author. New York: Lothrop, Lee & Shepard, 1986.
Peach Boy's courageous acts of kindness help rid his village of an ogre.

Sternberg, Martha, and Minoru Aoki. *Japan: A Week in Daisuke's World*. New York: Thomas Y. Crowell (Collier), 1973.
This information book gives a photographic essay about the daily life of a seven-year-old boy in Tokyo.

Uchida, Yoshiko. *Sumi and the Goat and the Tokyo Express*. Illustrated by Kazue Mizumura. New York: Charles Scribner's Sons, 1969.
Sumi is the only one who can get old Mr. Oda's goat to move from the path of the new Tokyo express.

———. *The Two Foolish Cats*. Illustrated by Margot Zemach. New York: Macmillan (Margaret K. McElderry Books), 1987.
Two cats ask a monkey to judge which of their rice cakes is largest, and the trickster makes the cakes equal by eating them both.

Watson, Jane Werner. *Japan: Islands of the Rising Sun*. Champaign, Ill.: Garrard, 1968.
This information book introduces young readers to the beautiful and busy islands of Japan and to the people at home, at work, at school, and at play.

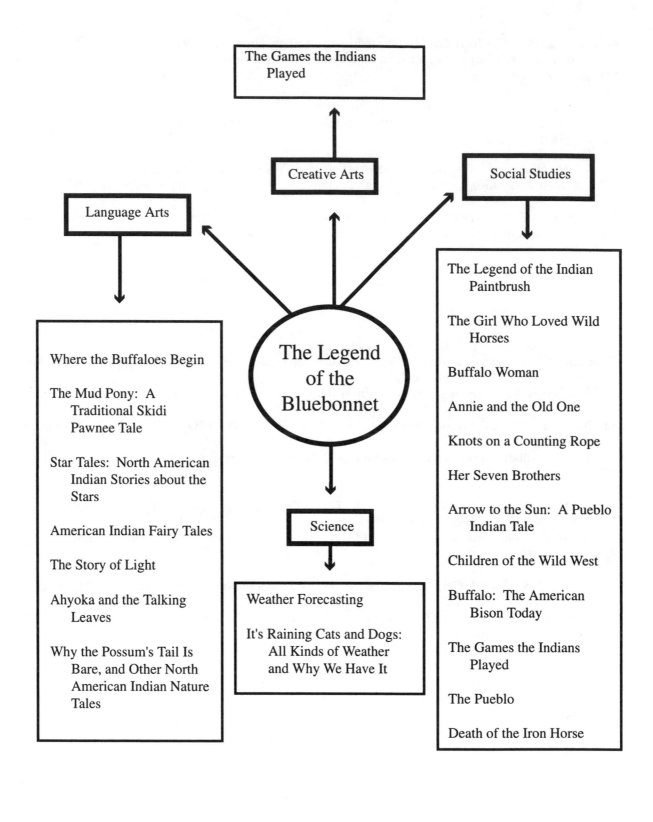

The Games the Indians Played

Creative Arts

Social Studies

Language Arts

The Legend of the Bluebonnet

The Legend of the Indian Paintbrush

The Girl Who Loved Wild Horses

Buffalo Woman

Annie and the Old One

Knots on a Counting Rope

Her Seven Brothers

Arrow to the Sun: A Pueblo Indian Tale

Children of the Wild West

Buffalo: The American Bison Today

The Games the Indians Played

The Pueblo

Death of the Iron Horse

Where the Buffaloes Begin

The Mud Pony: A Traditional Skidi Pawnee Tale

Star Tales: North American Indian Stories about the Stars

American Indian Fairy Tales

The Story of Light

Ahyoka and the Talking Leaves

Why the Possum's Tail Is Bare, and Other North American Indian Nature Tales

Science

Weather Forecasting

It's Raining Cats and Dogs: All Kinds of Weather and Why We Have It

10

The Legend of the Bluebonnet
ॐ

dePaola, Tomie. *The Legend of the Bluebonnet*. Illustrated by the author. New York: G. P. Putnam's Sons, 1983.

Genre: Folktale

Summary: A young Comanche Indian girl gives her only possession as a sacrifice for the Great Spirit to send rain. The ashes of her sacrifice became the beautiful flowers known as bluebonnets, which grow everywhere in Texas.

Content Areas: Language arts, math, science, social studies, and creative arts. This story could introduce a unit on Native Americans.

Brainstorming Starters:

Indians	Possessions
Families	Dolls
Buffalo	Spirits
Weather	Stories
Seasons	Folklore
Rain	Drums
Drought	Flowers
Loneliness	

Activities for Language Arts

"Most Valuable Possession"

After reading *The Legend of the Bluebonnet*, encourage students to think about which of their possessions is most valuable and why. Give the students a choice of writing a story about this most valuable possession or drawing a picture of it. Have students share their work in pairs or in small groups. After sharing, place the stories and drawings on the bulletin board.

"Rebus Stories"

Ask students to brainstorm how we communicate. Have them read *Ahyoka and the Talking Leaves*. List the students' ideas on the board or a chart. After discussing their ideas, call attention to writing as a means of communication. Ask students if they think She-Who-Is-Alone, a Comanche in *The Legend of the Bluebonnet*, used the same alphabet that we use today. After discussing what type alphabet she might have used, have students tell what they know about different alphabets. If students do not suggest symbols as a means of written communication, suggest that many people use symbols in writing. Have students suggest symbols that might be used for words. Have students write the word and the symbol on the board. Divide the class into groups and have them use symbols in writing a legend or a story about Native Americans. Have each group share its story with the class before placing the stories in a booklet for use in the reading center.

"Sharing Native American Legends"

Read aloud selections from *Star Tales: North American Indian Stories about the Stars* to the class. Discuss the role of legends and the influence of tribal history on Native American life. Divide the class into small groups for reading *Where the Buffaloes Begin*; *The Mud Pony: A Traditional Skidi Pawnee Tale*; *American Indian Fairy Tales*; *The Story of Light*; and *Why the Possum's Tail Is Bare, and other North American Indian Nature Tales*. Following the reading of one or more of these books, have the small groups retell a legend or give the history of a tribe. Encourage students to dress in Native American dress as they give these.

Activities for Math

"Math Drums"

Have small groups of students make two drums out of empty round boxes, such as oatmeal containers, and art supplies. Provide the groups with templates for drawing drums on construction paper. Have them cut out five drums and number the drums from one to five. On twenty-two other drums, write all possible addition problems (i.e., 1+0=__, 0+1=__, 1+1=__) for which the answers are one through five. Place the addition cut outs in one of the larger drums and the answer cut outs in the other large drum. Working in small groups, have students select a numeral from one drum and from the other drum select all possible addition problems that match the selected numeral.

"Tepee Match"

Cut out two sets of five-by-seven-inch cards with nine cards in each set. Number the cards one through nine. On the back of each card, draw the number of tepees indicated by the number you wrote on the front of the card. Working in pairs, have students match the cards that have the same number of tepees. Students can check their work by turning the cards over to see whether the numerals match. This can be varied by having students place the cards in order from the smallest number to the largest number, or by having one student lay down a card with the tepee side up and the partner laying down the matching card with the numeral side up.

Activities for Science

"Drought and Famine"

Read the books *Weather Forecasting* and *It's Raining Cats and Dogs: All Kinds of Weather and Why We Have It*. Write the words *drought* and *famine* on the chalkboard and introduce the terms through pictures. Display a sample research chart with three columns. The columns should be headed *What I Know*, *What I Want to Learn*, and *What I Learned*. Have small groups or pairs construct a chart about drought and famine. Provide encyclopedias, textbooks, pictures, and teacher-prepared fact sheets on drought and famine. Display the completed research charts in the classroom and discuss the results of drought. Following a discussion of the completed charts and drought conditions today, furnish students with world maps on which the students can color in or outline areas of drought in the world today. Display the maps with the research charts.

"Seasons Booklet"

After reading information books on seasons and weather, divide students into four groups to make booklets on seasons. Each group can brainstorm one season of the year and write its ideas on a chart. Distribute art supplies and magazine pictures to each group. Have the students find pictures that identify each season. Help students arrange the pictures on construction paper. Complete the booklet by placing a title on the outside cover. Place the booklets in the science center.

Activities for Social Studies

"State Flowers"

Discuss the flowers in *The Legend of the Bluebonnet* and *The Legend of the Indian Paintbrush*. Display pictures of several local states' official flower with the names of the states and flowers listed in random order on an accompanying chart. Encourage students to match the flowers with the correct state by research in trade books or encyclopedias. Divide the class into groups by having students select one of the state flowers. Have each group give the flower a new name and write a story about how the flower got to be the state flower. These accounts can be shared with the class through pictures or reader's theater.

"Legends and Folklore"

When studying folklore and legends, compare similar tales, such as *The Girl Who Loved Wild Horses* and *Buffalo Woman*; *Annie and the Old One* and *Knots on a Counting Rope*; or *Her Seven Brothers* and *Arrow to the Sun: A Pueblo Indian Tale*. Divide the class into three groups, each group made up of students who have read on or both books in a specific pair. The two books can be compared by making a chart that shows how each story is similar and different. Ask each group to share its completed chart with the class.

"Indian Life"

Share the pictures in *Children of the Wild West* or *Buffalo: The American Bison Today* and read *The Games the Indians Played, Death of the Iron Horse,* or *The Pueblo*. Encourage students to work individually or in pairs to make a tepee and tell a story about it; think of an Indian-type name for themselves and write or tell a story about how they got the name; collect pictures of Indian artifacts and write or tell about them; or research an Indian tribe and write or tell about the tribe. These projects will be shared with the class. Encourage students to dress in Indian costumes when giving their reports (see page 90).

Activities for Creative Arts

"Chant and Dance"

Divide the class into five groups to plan a presentation of *The Legend of the Bluebonnet*. One group can learn a game from *The Games the Indians Played* or write a chant similar to the one in the story. Another group can create a dance to a drumbeat. Provide heavy cardboard, feathers, paints, beads, and other supplies for another group to create a most valuable possession. Another group can make headbands from art supplies for the shaman and dancers. The fifth group can use blue ink and art supplies to make bluebonnets from thumbprints. Invite parents or friends to an Indian show-and-tell day so that students can share their projects.

Bulletin Boards

"Bluebonnets"

Prepare the background of the bulletin board by having one group cut hills from green construction paper. Staple the hills into place on the board. Have another group draw white clouds and the sun on the background paper. Draw in approximately fifty green flower stems with a marker. Write the word *Bluebonnets* on a cloud and place it at the top of the board. Each student can create bluebonnets on one or two of the stems with thumbprints made from blue ink.

"Most Valuable Possession"

Place the phrase *Most Valuable Possession* in the center of the bulletin board. Fasten the pictures and stories from the language arts activity "Most Valuable Possession" on the bulletin board.

Related Books

Baker, Olaf. *Where the Buffaloes Begin*. Illustrated by Stephen Gammell. New York: Frederic Warne, 1981.
    Little Wolf, a courageous boy, tries to find the lake where the buffaloes begin.

Branley, Franklyn M. *It's Raining Cats and Dogs: All Kinds of Weather and Why We Have It*. Illustrated by True Kelley. Boston: Houghton Mifflin, 1987.
    This information book offers folklore and information about rain, snow, smog, lightning, hurricanes, tornadoes, and clouds.

Cohen, Caron Lee. *The Mud Pony: A Traditional Skidi Pawnee Tale*. Illustrated by Shonto Begay. New York: Scholastic, 1988.
    The spirit of Mother Earth in the shape of a horse made from clay comes to a boy.

Compton, Margaret. *American Indian Fairy Tales*. Illustrated by Lorence Bjorklund. New York: Dodd, Mead, 1971.
    Authentic legends told by Pacific Coast, Midwest, and New England tribesmen.

Connolly, James. *Why the Possum's Tail Is Bare, and Other North American Indian Nature Tales*. Illustrated by Andrea Adams. Owings Mills, Md.: Stemmer House/Barbara Holdridge Books, 1985.
    The author gives a brief history of the North American Indians represented in these stories, as well as background information on each of the stories.

dePaola, Tomie. *The Legend of the Bluebonnet*. Illustrated by the author. New York: G. P. Putnam's Sons, 1983.
    A young Comanche Indian girl gives her only possession as a sacrifice for the Great Spirit to send rain. The ashes of her sacrifice became the beautiful flowers known as bluebonnets, which grow everywhere in Texas.

———. *The Legend of the Indian Paintbrush*. Illustrated by the author. New York: G. P. Putnam's Sons, 1988.
    This legend tells how a wildflower, the Indian paintbrush, got its name.

Freedman, Russell. *Children of the Wild West*. New York: Clarion Books, 1983.
    The photographs offer a wealth of information on the schools, homes, work, and play of children in the nineteenth-century American West, although the text is advanced.

Gibbons, Gail. *Weather Forecasting*. Illustrated by the author. New York: Four Winds Press, 1987.
    This brightly illustrated book tells about weather and forecasting during the four seasons.

Goble, Paul. *Buffalo Woman*. Illustrated by the author. Scarsdale, N.Y.: Bradbury Press, 1984.
    This legend from the Plains Indians tells about a buffalo that turns into a beautiful girl.

———. *Death of the Iron Horse*. Illustrated by the author. Scarsdale, N.Y.: Bradbury Press, 1987.
    This story, based on an actual Cheyenne attack on a steam train, is told from the Native American point of view.

———. *The Girl Who Loved Wild Horses*. Illustrated by the author. Scarsdale, N.Y.: Bradbury Press, 1978. (Caldecott Medal)
    The author tells the story of an American Indian girl and her love of horses.

———. *Her Seven Brothers*. Illustrated by the author. Scarsdale, N.Y.: Bradbury Press, 1988.
    A Cheyenne legend tells of the origin of the Big Dipper.

Laverne, Sigmund. *The Games the Indians Played*. Illustrated with photographs. New York: Dodd, Mead, 1974.
    This information book describes recreational pastimes of American Indians and Eskimos.

McDermott, Gerald. *Arrow to the Sun: A Pueblo Indian Tale*. Illustrated by the author. New York: Viking, 1974.
    This legend is the story of a search by a young Indian boy for his father, the Sun.

Martin, Bill Jr., and John Archambault. *Knots on a Counting Rope*. Illustrated by Ted Rand. Salt Lake City, Utah: Henry Holt, 1987.
    A Native American's grandfather tries to help the boy grow strong and independent despite the boy's blindness.

Mayo, Gretchen Will. *Star Tales: North American Indian Stories About the Stars*. Illustrated by the author. New York: Walker, 1987.
    Fourteen Indian legends about the stars, from various North American Indians, are retold. These make good read-aloud selections.

Miles, Miska. *Annie and the Old One*. Illustrated by Peter Parnall. Boston: Little, Brown, 1971.
    A young Navajo girl realizes her grandmother is dying and tries to put off the inevitable.

Patent, Dorothy Hinshaw. *Buffalo: The American Bison Today*. Photographs by William Munoz. New York: Clarion Books, 1986.
Although the text is advanced, the photographs give a true picture of the life of a buffalo.

Roop, Peter and Connie Roop. *Ahyoka and the Talking Leaves*. Illustrated by Yoshi Miyake. New York: Lothrop, Lee & Shepard, 1992.
A Cherokee girl and her father must leave their home in their search for a written Cherokee language.

Roth, Susan L. *The Story of Light*. New York: Morrow Junior Books, 1990.
This story tells how animals brought light into the world.

Yue, Charlotte, and David Yue. *The Pueblo*. Boston: Houghton Mifflin, 1986.
This information book gives a detailed account of Pueblo Indian daily life, customs, history, and dwellings from ancient times to the present day.

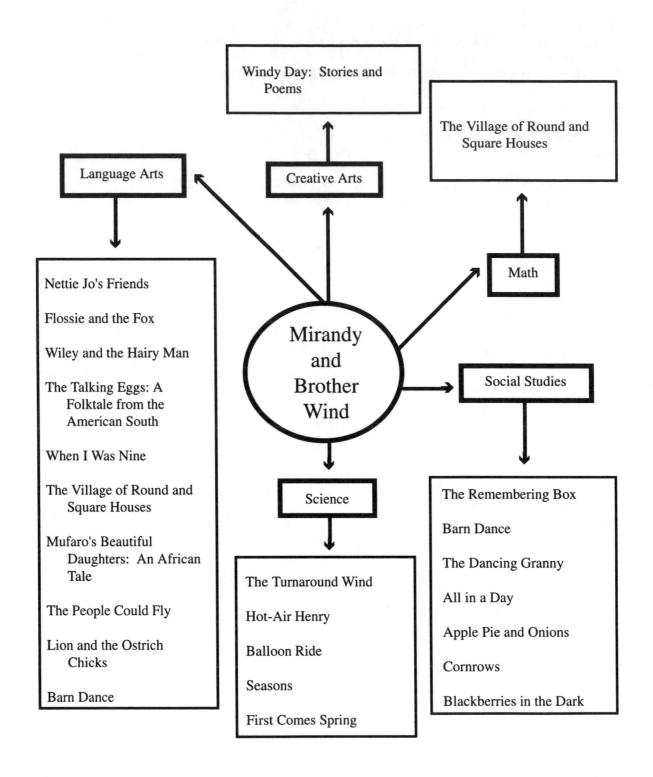

Windy Day: Stories and
Poems

The Village of Round and
Square Houses

Language Arts

Creative Arts

Math

Mirandy
and
Brother
Wind

Social Studies

Nettie Jo's Friends

Flossie and the Fox

Wiley and the Hairy Man

The Talking Eggs: A
Folktale from the
American South

When I Was Nine

The Village of Round and
Square Houses

Mufaro's Beautiful
Daughters: An African
Tale

The People Could Fly

Lion and the Ostrich
Chicks

Barn Dance

Science

The Turnaround Wind

Hot-Air Henry

Balloon Ride

Seasons

First Comes Spring

The Remembering Box

Barn Dance

The Dancing Granny

All in a Day

Apple Pie and Onions

Cornrows

Blackberries in the Dark

11

Mirandy and Brother Wind

৯

McKissack, Patricia C. *Mirandy and Brother Wind*. Illustrated by Jerry Pinkney. New York: Alfred A. Knopf (Borzoi Books), 1988. (Caldecott Honor)

Genre: Folktale

Summary: Mirandy tries to capture the wind to make it her partner in the Junior Cakewalk so that she can win first prize.

Content Areas: Language arts, math, science, social studies, and creative arts. This book could be used to introduce a social studies unit on various cultures or multiculturalism.

Brainstorming Starters:

Spring	Barns
Wind	Farm animals
Dancing	Milking
Cakewalk	Conjure
Family relationships	Scarves
Family history	Friendship
Family customs	

Activities for Language Arts

"Flannel Board Character Tales"

Begin a study of folktales by presenting *Mirandy and Brother Wind* to the class in a storytelling session. Following the storytelling session, have students discuss the characteristics of folktales and identify those characteristics in *Mirandy and Brother Wind*. On the reading table display *Nettie Jo's Friends* and *Flossie and the Fox* along with other folktales, such as *Wiley and the Hairy Man, The Talking Eggs: A Folktale from the American South, When I Was Nine, The Village of Round and Square Houses, Mufaro's Beautiful Daughters: An African Tale,* and the folktale collections *The People Could Fly* and *Lion and the Ostrich Chicks*. Encourage students to read books from the table and select one story that could be used for storytelling. Have students draw a large, round circle on a sheet of paper and divide it into eight equal parts. Have students select eight events from their folktale and write a one-phrase summary of each event (in the order they occurred) in the sections of the circle. Remind students that the story circle can help them remember the story when retelling it. After students have read several folk stories, have them use felt or interfacing fabric to make small flannel-board characters from the stories. The completed pieces can be placed in a box. Have each student select one figure from the box. Divide the class into cooperative groups so that all characters from one story are together. The groups can think of new stories about the characters and place the story events on a story wheel. After practicing storytelling, the students can tell the new story and manipulate the characters on the flannel board.

"Oral History"

After reading several folktales and discussing the role of oral history in preserving stories from the past, have students invite grandparents or other adults to the classroom to share stories that were passed down to them. Ask each guest to share several stories related to marriages, births, deaths, folk remedies, games, or superstitions. After each story, allow students to ask questions. As a follow-up activity, have students recall some of the stories and form groups to write a story that could be passed down. Have each group share its story with the class. Encourage students to collect family stories from other older adults, such as friends, relatives, or neighbors. Encourage students to write about one story they heard. Have students form groups to revise their stories and then write the revised story in their neatest handwriting. Finished products can be displayed in the hallway or outside the classroom on a bulletin board.

"Story Writing"

After reading several folktales, have each student select a character from one of the stories and imagine that they are going to spend a complete day together. Have the student list several events that might occur during the day and write a short story about what it was like to spend a day with the character. Encourage students to illustrate their stories before placing them on display.

"Compare and Contrast"

After reading *Barn Dance*, *Nettie Jo's Friends*, *Flossie and the Fox*, and *Mufaro's Beautiful Daughters: An African Tale*, have students write about the books in their journals. Divide the class into cooperative groups for comparing and contrasting the family stories of McKissack and *Mufaro's Beautiful Daughters*. Ask students to list ways the stories are alike and different. Have students compare and defend their findings.

"Folktale Party"

Plan a party in which students will come as their favorite folktale character. Students can make costumes by decorating old clothes with crayons, paints, and beads, or they can use costumes that have been collected for classroom use. Have each student prepare a short presentation about the character's folktale. Group students by the tale selected and have them give all presentations about one story together. After the presentations, serve punch and cake.

Activities for Math

"Advertisement for Cakewalk"

After reading *Mirandy and Brother Wind*, group students to make signs or pamphlets advertising the cakewalk. Encourage each group to illustrate its advertisement. Remind students to include the price of the punch, which was to be sold at the cakewalk. Have each group figure how much it would have to charge for a cup of punch to make a profit. Tell students the cost of ingredients for the punch and how many cups the recipe will make. The group assignment is to determine a price so that the group can make a one-cent profit on each cup of punch. Ask the groups to estimate how many recipes of punch will be needed for 50 and 100 people. Each group can share its advertisement and the results of its calculations. Write all calculations on the chalkboard for comparison. If the calculations differ, help the students determine the correct one.

"Milk Containers"

After reading *Mirandy and Brother Wind*, call attention to the section of the book related to milking. Allow students to describe their experiences with milking, visiting dairies, and buying milk. Introduce the words *pint* and *quart* by showing milk cartons with the correct capacity written on a card attached to the carton. After discussing which is larger, have students estimate how many cups are in a pint. Have a volunteer fill a measuring cup with one cup of water and pour the water into the pint carton. Ask another volunteer to add another cup of water. Following this, ask students to estimate how many cups and pints are in one quart. Have volunteers demonstrate how many cups and pints it takes to fill a quart container. Ask students how many cups are needed to fill two, three, four, and five pints and how many pints are needed to fill two, three, four, and five quarts. Display several containers of various sizes, such as thermos bottles, measuring cups, and large glasses. Ask volunteers to estimate how many cups of water it will take to fill one of the containers. The students can then fill the containers to verify their estimates. Have students collect pictures of cup, pint, and quart containers to display in the math center.

"Shapes"

After reading *The Village of Round and Square Houses*, display a number of three-dimensional objects, including spheres and cubes. Have students describe each object by telling whether or not it has points or curves. Place several items in the shape of cubes, spheres, cones, and rectangles in a bag. Have volunteers feel in the bag and tell which object on display is the same shape as the one they are feeling. Students can verify their guesses by removing the object from the bag. Have students find round or square objects in the classroom. Have students bring round or square objects to class, such as balls of various sizes, boxes, and counting blocks. Give students the choice of drawing houses using only squares and circles or finding round or square objects in magazines and cutting out and mounting the pictures on construction paper. The finished projects can be displayed in the classroom.

Activities for Science

"What Is Air?"

In preparation for discussing air, read *The Turnaround Wind* and show pictures of what happened when the wild wind descended. Suggest that the wind is moving air and ask students where air is found or what is its source. Ask them whether air is present in boxes and bags. Have students blow up balloons or clear plastic bags. Ask them to feel the bags. Discuss what is in the bags and what happens when the bag or balloon is touched. Have students open the bags or release the balloons. Ask if they could see the air. Ask students to name the senses that tell us air is present. Have students fold a piece of paper to form a fan and wave the fan in front of their faces. Discuss the result. Ask what things we can see being moved by air; show pictures of flags, wind chimes, and pinwheels. Show the class different kinds of air pumps and ask how they work. State that scuba divers wear oxygen tanks to breathe. Have students identify other jobs or situations (i.e., astronauts) that require special ways of obtaining air or special needs for air. Divide the class into groups to research this topic. Have them find or draw pictures to show the results of their research. Give each group an opportunity to report its findings.

"Moving Air"

Have students make a spinner by placing a heavy strip of cardboard on the top of a pencil eraser and sticking a straight pin into the eraser to hold the cardboard in place. Walk outside to see if the wind is blowing. Try to determine its direction using the spinner. Read *Hot-Air Henry* and *Balloon Ride* to the class and encourage students to tell what they know about how the burner heats the air in the hot air balloon. Have class members relate any experiences they have had with airplanes or hot air balloons. Ask students to research information on how hot air balloons work. After discussing what was learned, ask the students to write stories about experiences with air or how it might feel to ride in a hot air balloon. Share the stories. Provide materials for students to make windsocks by tying three streamers of one-by-eighteen-inch crepe paper to a ring about four inches in diameter. Move the windsock back and forth to see how it reacts.

"Strong Winds"

Begin this activity by reading *Seasons* and *First Comes Spring* and discussing springtime activities related to the wind. Help the class arrive at a definition of wind as moving air. Ask if any students have ever seen weather balloons. Explain that they are used to determine wind speed and direction. Following this discussion, have students make suggestions about what high winds can do. Assist students as they research and define tornadoes as strong surface winds and hurricanes as storms with high winds. Form groups to research dangerous weather and rules for safety in such weather. Have the groups role-play a weatherman giving a forecast. Have each forecaster read the group's list of safety rules for storms. Have the students compare and discuss safety rules. Have groups make collages or a book illustrating wind and windy day activities.

"Wind Power"

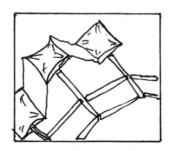

Ask the class to name things that are powered by wind. Have groups research things that are powered by wind, such as sailboats and kites. Have each group invent something that is powered by wind. Ask the groups to draw pictures of their inventions and share them with the class. Then show and read *The Turnaround Wind* and allow students to try to make an upside-down design like those in the book. Share the results. Put all of the pictures together for a class upside-down book.

Activities for Social Studies

"Compare and Contrast"

Display *The Remembering Box, Barn Dance, The Dancing Granny,* and *All in a Day.* Ask students to read one of the books. Have the students fold a sheet of paper in half. On one half have the students write *then*; on the other half, *now.* Ask the students to compare the pictures, dress, buildings, actions, and language in the books. In the column labeled *then,* have the students write information gleaned from the books they read; in the column labeled *now,* have them record information about today. Group all students who read the same book. Have the students in each group compare their papers. Have each group then compile and refine its work and present one report to the class.

"Family Traditions and History"

After reading *Apple Pie and Onions, Blackberries in the Dark,* and *Cornrows,* have students try to find information about their ancestral or cultural origins. Have students collect family stories and traditions that have been passed down, focusing on holiday traditions. Have students write a family story. Put all of the stories together in a book.

Activities for Creative Arts

"Design a Kite"

After reading *Windy Day: Stories and Poems,* provide materials for students to design and make a kite. The section on *Kites* in an encyclopedia has directions for making kites and safety rules. Discuss safety rules for flying kites and how to make a kite fly. Take the kites outside on a windy day and let the students try to fly their kites.

"Diorama"

Divide the class into groups to make dioramas of the major events in *Mirandy and Brother Wind.* Shoe boxes or cardboard boxes can be used for the scenes; pipe cleaners, felt, and other materials can be used for making the people. Twigs, craft dough, and cotton balls can be used for other parts of the diorama. Arrange the dioramas in proper sequence for viewing.

"Dramatization"

Divide the class into groups for making puppets to dramatize a part of one of the folktales. First, each group should select a scene to dramatize and write a brief skit. Allow groups to (1) make puppets by drawing a character, cutting it out, and gluing the figure to a craft stick or (2) make paper plate puppets. Have each group present its dramatization. Have the class discuss other scenes or stories that could be dramatized.

Bulletin Boards

"Shaped Houses"

Place a large square and a large circle in the center of the bulletin board with the phrase *Our Class Designs Square and Round Houses* as the heading. Have the students glue the house designs they made in the math activity "Shapes" on large construction paper that has been cut to be a square or circle. Place the pictures on the bulletin board.

"Windy Day Activities"

Place the phrase *Windy Day Activities* in the center of the bulletin board. Provide art supplies for students to construct small kites with strings attached. After constructing and attaching the kites to the bulletin board, have the students think of windy day activities. Have the students write their ideas on small pieces of paper, which can be glued on the strings attached to the kites.

Related Books

Anno, Mitsumasa. *All in a Day*. New York: Putnam, 1986.
    The brief text and illustrations reveal the similarities and differences in the lives of children in eight different countries.

Bang, Molly. *Wiley and the Hairy Man*. New York: Macmillan, 1976.
    This story, adapted from an African folktale, tells how Wiley becomes a "conjure man" to outwit the hairy man.

Bauer, Caroline F. *Windy Day: Stories and Poems*. Illustrated by Dirk Zimmer. New York: J. B. Lippincott, 1988.
    This is an anthology of words and rhythms that evoke a variety of images about wind.

Bryan, Ashley. *The Dancing Granny*. Retold and illustrated by Ashley Bryan. New York: Macmillan (Aladdin Books), 1977.
    The trickster Spider Ananse gets Granny started dancing but gets himself tricked.

———. *Lion and the Ostrich Chicks*. Retold and illustrated by Ashley Bryan. New York: Atheneum, 1986.
    This book includes four traditional tales told by four tribes of Africa.

Calhoun, Mary. *Hot-Air Henry*. Illustrated by Erick Ingraham. New York: Mulberry Books, 1981.
    A Siamese cat takes an adventure in a hot air balloon.

Caseley, Judith. *Apple Pie and Onions*. Illustrated by the author. New York: Greenwillow Books, 1987.
A grandmother helps her granddaughter find her family roots and traditions.

Clifford, Eth. *The Remembering Box*. Illustrated by Donna Diamond. Boston: Houghton Mifflin, 1985.
Joshua's grandmother's small objects from her Remembering Box help him understand his Jewish roots.

Goennel, Heidi. *Seasons*. Illustrated by the author. Boston: Little, Brown, 1986.
The text and beautifully designed paintings depict favorite activities for each season.

Grifalconi, Ann. *The Village of Round and Square Houses*. Boston: Little, Brown, 1986. (Caldecott Honor)
An African folktale about why in one village the men live in square houses and the women live in round ones.

Hamilton, Virginia. *The People Could Fly*. Illustrated by Leo Dillon and Diane Dillon. New York: Alfred A. Knopf (Borzoi Books), 1985.
These are retold African-American folktales.

Jukes, Mavis. *Blackberries in the Dark*. New York: Alfred A. Knopf, 1985.
After his grandfather's death, a young boy and his grandmother discover a new relationship.

Lobel, Arnold. *The Turnaround Wind*. Illustrated by the author. New York: Harper & Row, 1988.
This book shows what happens to the characters when a wild wind descends.

McKissack, Patricia. *Flossie and the Fox*. Illustrated by Rachel Isadora. New York: Dial Books for Young Readers, 1986.
A wily fox meets his match in a bold little girl he encounters in the woods.

———. *Mirandy and Brother Wind*. Illustrated by Jerry Pinkney. New York: Alfred A. Knopf (Borzoi Books), 1988.
Mirandy tries to capture the wind to make it her partner in the Junior Cakewalk so that she can win first prize.

———. *Nettie Jo's Friends*. Illustrated by Scott Cook. New York: Alfred A. Knopf (Borzoi Books), 1989.
Nettie Jo looks for a needle to sew her doll's dress, but the three animals she asks to help her surprise her in the end.

Martin, Bill Jr., and John Archambault. *Barn Dance*. Illustrated by Ted Rand. New York: Henry Holt, 1986.
A boy tries to find out what the owl means when it says, "There's magic in the air." In the process he finds a magical barn dance in full swing.

Mott, Evelyn Clarke. *Balloon Ride*. Photographs by the author. New York: Walker, 1991.
This book tells the details of how to operate a hot air balloon.

Rockwell, Anne. *First Comes Spring*. Illustrated by the author. New York: Thomas Y. Crowell, 1985.
Beautiful illustrations show spring activities, such as putting up a birdhouse and plowing fields.

San Souci, Robert D. *The Talking Eggs: A Folktale from the American South.* Illustrated by Jerry Pinkney. New York: Dial Books for Young Readers, 1989. (Caldecott Honor)
A folktale in which good is rewarded over evil.

Steptoe, John. *Mufaro's Beautiful Daughters: An African Tale.* Illustrated by the author. New York: Lothrop, Lee & Shepard, 1987.
A beautifully illustrated story tells the fate of two sisters, one kind, the other selfish.

Stevenson, James. *When I Was Nine.* New York: Greenwillow Books, 1986.
This account of a childhood summer introduces journal-keeping and autobiographical writing activities.

Yarborough, Camille. *Cornrows.* New York: Coward, McCann & Geoghegan, 1979.
This is the story of the origin of the African hair-braiding technique called cornrows.

Animal Stories

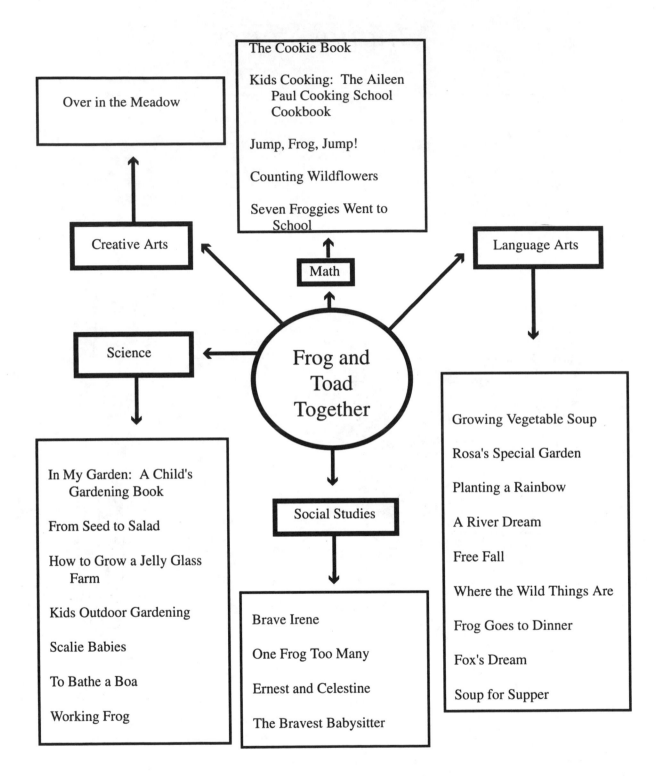

Over in the Meadow

The Cookie Book

Kids Cooking: The Aileen Paul Cooking School Cookbook

Jump, Frog, Jump!

Counting Wildflowers

Seven Froggies Went to School

Creative Arts

Math

Language Arts

Frog and Toad Together

Science

Social Studies

In My Garden: A Child's Gardening Book

From Seed to Salad

How to Grow a Jelly Glass Farm

Kids Outdoor Gardening

Scalie Babies

To Bathe a Boa

Working Frog

Brave Irene

One Frog Too Many

Ernest and Celestine

The Bravest Babysitter

Growing Vegetable Soup

Rosa's Special Garden

Planting a Rainbow

A River Dream

Free Fall

Where the Wild Things Are

Frog Goes to Dinner

Fox's Dream

Soup for Supper

12

Frog and Toad Together

Lobel, Arnold. *Frog and Toad Together*. Illustrated by the author. New York: Harper & Row, 1972.

Genre: Animal stories

Summary: Five humorous stories describe the further adventures of these caring friends.

Content Areas: Language arts, math, science, social studies, and creative arts. This book can be used to introduce a science or language arts unit on gardening or a math unit on counting and measuring.

Brainstorming Starters:

Making lists   Friendship
Gardening   Dragon
Flower seeds   Giant
Cookies   Snake
Bird food   Hawk
Willpower   Avalanche
Bravery   Dream

Activities for Language Arts

"Vegetable and Plant Match"

Read *Frog and Toad Together* aloud. Have students read *Growing Vegetable Soup*, *Rosa's Special Garden*, *Soup for Supper*, or *Planting a Rainbow*. Have students list vegetables or flowers that they would like to plant. (Inventive spelling is in order.) Have each student fold a sheet of paper to make twelve or sixteen squares and in each square draw or paste pictures of the plants from their lists. Write the name of each plant on slips of paper. Distribute these to the students and have them match the words with the pictures. Students may swap game cards in an attempt to identify more words. This activity could be expanded by giving each student a blank booklet shaped like a vegetable or flower. Students would draw or glue a picture of a vegetable or flower on each blank page and label the pictures or write sentences beneath them.

"My Dream"

After reading *A River Dream*, *Fox's Dream*, *Free Fall*, or *Where the Wild Things Are*, have students write about, tape record, or draw a picture of a dream they have had. Drawings and stories could be placed in a booklet in the reading center and tapes placed in the listening center.

"Picture Book"

Introduce the development of a wordless picture book or picture story book by sharing *Frog Goes to Dinner* with the class. After discussing Frog's adventures, have students suggest other places Frog could go, such as a football game, circus, school, or dentist. Divide the class into several cooperative groups to make a picture book or picture story book. Provide sheets of paper for the book and art supplies for the illustrations. Tell the groups to decide where Frog will go and what will happen to him. After planning, the groups can draw their illustrations and add any words needed to tell the story. Stress the importance of every person in the group making a contribution to the story. After the books are completed, each group can share its book with the class. Place the completed books in the reading center.

Activities for Math

"Cooking"

Have students read directions for a favorite cookie recipe from *The Cookie Book* or *Kids Cooking: The Aileen Paul Cooking School Cookbook*. Introduce vocabulary terms related to cooking (i.e., ingredients, teaspoon, cup) through a brainstorming session. Select recipes to prepare in class. (You might want to focus on recipes that require no cooking or use of sharp knives, such as a salad made from canned fruit or bread dough that can be left to rise during the afternoon and then taken home to be baked.) Ask students to provide some of the ingredients for cooking. In preparation for cooking, the students can practice measuring ingredients. Water, beans, sand, and rice can be used for measuring and for comparing the capacity of containers. Groups of students can then mix and prepare a recipe. All of the finished products could be sampled by the class. A booklet of favorite recipes can be prepared by each class member. The booklets would first be shared in class and then given to or shared with a parent or friend.

"Counting Wildflowers Game"

Read the book *Counting Wildflowers* to the class. Divide the class into groups. Have each group draw several small pictures of the wildflowers shown in the book. Have them cut the pictures out and glue them to a sheet of drawing paper (see page 107). Have them write the word *Start* before the first flower and *Winner* after the last flower. Prepare a set of addition and subtraction problems for each group on three-by-five-inch cards. Each student can make a marker—a small bug or frog—from scraps of construction paper. Have each student pick a problem card and supply an answer. If the answer is correct, the student moves the marker to the first flower. If the answer is incorrect, the card is placed at the bottom of the stack and the student does not move the marker. The game continues until someone reaches the winning space. The game can be repeated several times, with the winner from the previous game serving as the expert when there is a question about an answer.

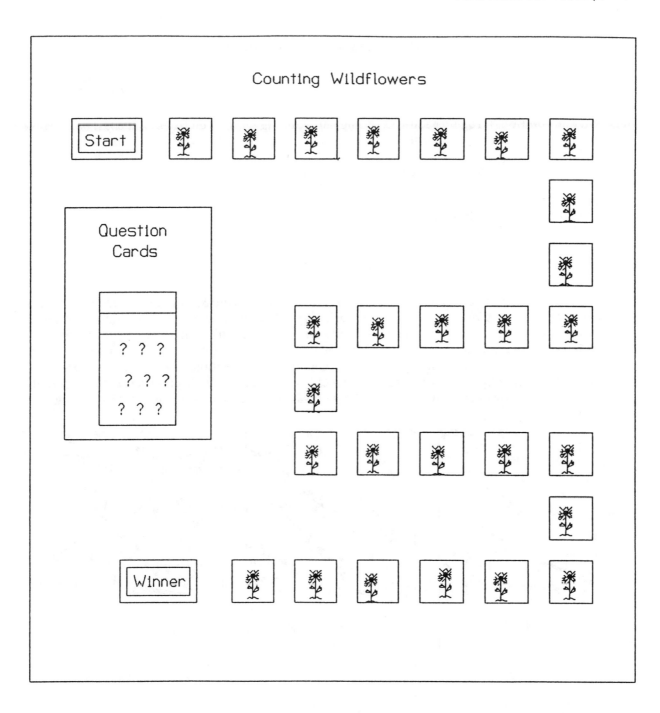

"The Froggies' Adventures"

Read *Seven Froggies Went to School* and *Jump, Frog, Jump!* and discuss the antics of the frogs. Divide the class into groups to make counting books about the adventures of the frogs. Give each group seven blank sheets of paper and art supplies to make a counting book with one frog on the first page and one additional frog on each succeeding page, ending with seven frogs on the last page. Have the students draw the frogs going to a different place (such as a restaurant or the library) on each page. After the groups have completed the counting books, have them exchange books. After the groups have shared the books, place them in the math area.

Activities for Science

"Planning a Garden"

After reading *In My Garden: A Child's Gardening Book*, *From Seed to Salad*, *How to Grow a Jelly Glass Farm*, and *Kids Outdoor Gardening*, groups of students can plan a vegetable garden for the school campus. (If no outside space is available, plant the garden in pots or paper cups on a window ledge.) Have students measure the selected garden plot. Following preparation of the garden soil by the class, select and plant seeds. Have students write directions for caring for the garden. Have students observe the garden several times weekly and record their observations in their journals. For each entry, students can draw a picture of what was observed and write about the drawing.

"Reptiles"

Introduce a study of reptiles by asking if any of the students have ever had a frog or snake for a pet. Allow time for several students to describe their pet and how they took care of it. Show pictures of reptiles. Include pictures that show reptiles in natural and zoo settings. Let students tell what they know about them. Ask the students to look at each picture to determine where the reptiles can be found. Share the books *Scalie Babies*, *To Bathe a Boa*, and *Working Frog* with the students. Discuss the information presented in *Scalie Babies* and *Working Frog*. Ask students why you should not bathe a snake.

Divide the class into groups to research reptiles. Have them find information on different kinds of reptiles, the characteristics of each kind, where they are found in nature, if they walk or swim, and what each kind eats. Have each group collect or draw pictures of its findings and write the facts on a chart. Have each group share its findings with the class and place its chart in the science center.

Activities for Social Studies

"Feelings Role-Play"

To work together, students must be aware of others' feelings. Read *One Frog Too Many* and *Ernest and Celestine*. Discuss feelings with students. Following the discussion, look at pictures depicting various feelings and ask what feeling is being expressed. Divide the class into groups and give each group a different situation involving feelings to role-play. These might include getting a new pet, losing a prized possession, or losing a contest to a friend.

"Class Experts: Learning from Others"

Show pictures of a child learning to do something, such as ride a bicycle or bake cookies. Have students describe how they felt when learning a difficult task and tell who helped them learn. Ask the class to think about things that must be learned. List their ideas on the board; encourage them to include ideas such as taking care of a younger sibling or learning to accept change. Read *The Bravest Babysitter* and *Brave Irene*. Have students identify the teacher and the learner and tell what was learned. Divide the class into pairs to think of something that they could help someone else learn or a problem that they could help someone overcome. Give each student a blank sheet of paper with the outline of a boy or girl on it. Have each child write his or her partner's name on the paper and then write a description of what that person could teach someone else. As the pairs complete the assignment, have them place the sheets in a booklet titled *Class Experts* on the reading table.

Activities for Creative Arts

"Song Writing"

After reading *Over in the Meadow*, form collaborative groups to write a song or rhythm activity about friends, frogs, animals, or gardening. Have groups prepare pictures, dioramas, or puppets to use in presenting the song or activity to the class. Have each group would lead the class in singing the song or participating in the rhythm activity.

Bulletin Boards

"Words from a Garden"

Cover the bulletin board with light blue paper for background (see page 111). Across the top of the board, place the phrase *Words from a Garden*. Cut three large green stems from construction paper and glue them to the board. Glue strips of green construction paper across the bottom of the board to serve as grass. Affix two large envelopes to the bottom corners of the board. Glue a round yellow disk above the center of each stem to serve as the center of flowers, which will be constructed by students. Write the letters *n*, *e*, and *s* in the center of each disk. From white construction paper, cut out approximately forty daisy petals. On half of the daisy petals, write these words: *mushroom, peppers, apple, onion, grape, squash, watermelon, potato, peas, broccoli, turnips, peach, pineapple, lemon, corn, bean, asparagus, peanuts, carrots, olives, dates, pumpkin, orange,* and *cabbage*. Place these petals in one envelope on the bulletin board. Place the blank petals in the other envelope on the board. Allow small groups of students to go to the board and place petals on the plants. The letter on the center of the disk determines which daisy petal goes on that plant. For the center containing the letter *n*, the petals should be ones bearing words that end with *n* (i.e., bean, lemon). If students think of another vegetable or fruit that ends with *n* (i.e., raisin) it could be written on one of the blank daisy petals and that petal affixed to the appropriate daisy.

"Make a Word"

Cover the bulletin board with colorful paper (see page 112). Place the title *Make a Word* across the top of the board. Glue or draw pictures of vegetables, plants, or animals on four-inch squares, and glue the squares across the board in rows. Draw a line on several sheets of paper and place one sheet under each picture. Write alphabet letters on small pieces of construction paper; make enough letters to spell each item pictured. Make a large bowl and spoon from cardboard or boxes and place on a table in front of the bulletin board. Put the letters in the bowl. In groups of three or four, students may select ten letters from the bowl. If a word matching one of the pictures can be made, the student places the letters on the line below the appropriate picture. Unused letters are returned to the bowl, and another group gets a chance to try. This activity continues until all pictures have been labeled.

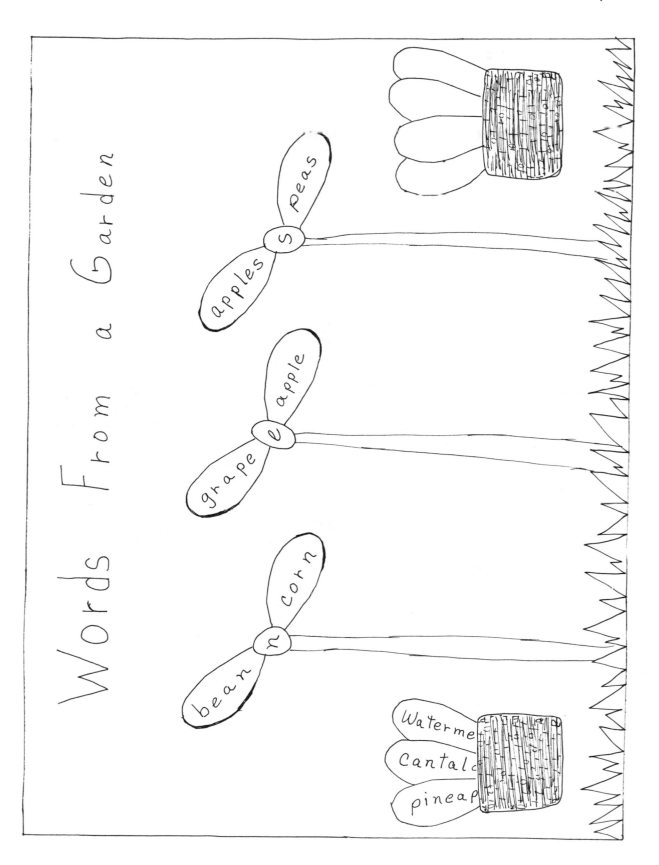

Words From a Garden

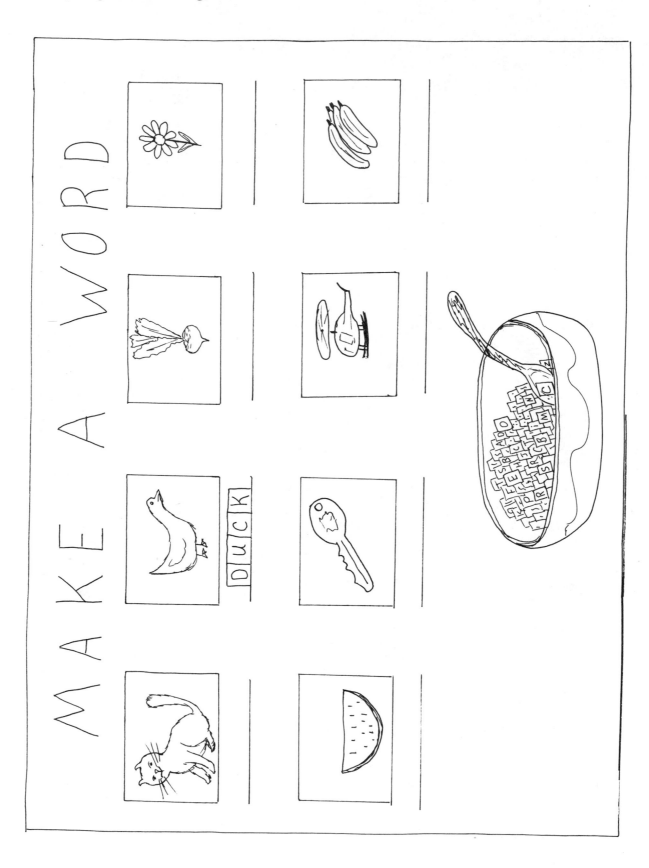

Related Books

Duke, Kate. *Seven Froggies Went to School*. Illustrated by the author. Bergenfield, N.J.: E. P. Dutton, 1985.
The antics of seven froggies at school are brightly illustrated.

Ehlert, Lois. *Growing Vegetable Soup*. Illustrated by the author. New York: Harcourt Brace Jovanovich, 1987.
A child helps his father grow vegetables for soup.

————. *Planting a Rainbow*. Illustrated by the author. New York: Harcourt Brace Jovanovich, 1988.
The bright illustrations show colors, seeds, and plants and tell how plants grow.

Fife, Dale H. *Rosa's Special Garden*. Illustrated by Marie De John. New York: Albert Whitman, 1985.
A story about a family planting a garden tells how the four-year-old Rosa gardens her own special plot.

Greenberg, Barbara. *The Bravest Babysitter*. Illustrated by Diane Paterson. New York: Dial Books for Young Readers, 1977.
A baby-sitter's young charge helps her overcome her fears of thunder and lightning.

Johnson, Hanna Lyons. *From Seed to Salad*. Illustrated with photographs. New York: Lothrop, Lee & Shepard, 1978.
A guide to gardening gives tips.

Johnston, Ginny, and Judy Cutchins. *Scalie Babies*. New York: Morrow Junior Books, 1988.
A variety of baby reptiles, including snakes, are shown as they struggle to survive and reach maturity.

Kalan, Robert. *Jump, Frog, Jump!* Illustrated by Byron Barton. New York: Mulberry Books, 1981.
This is a cumulative tale about a frog that tries to catch a fly without getting caught itself.

Kudrna, C. Imbior. *To Bathe a Boa*. Illustrated by the author. Minneapolis, Minn.: Carolrhoda Books, 1986.
A little boy wants to give his pet boa a bath, but the snake has other ideas and hides from him.

Langstaff, John. *Over in the Meadow*. Illustrated by Feodor Rojankovsky. New York: Harcourt Brace Jovanovich, 1957.
This story is based on an old animal counting song.

Lobel, Arnold. *Frog and Toad Together*. Illustrated by the author. New York: Harper & Row, 1972.
Five humorous stories describe the further adventures of these caring friends.

McMillan, Bruce. *Counting Wildflowers*. Photographs by the author. New York: Lothrop, Lee & Shepard, 1986.
Numbers from one to twenty are presented within a framework of color identification and wildflower recognition.

Mandry, Kathy. *How to Grow a Jelly Glass Farm.* Illustrated by Joe Toto. New York: Pantheon Books, 1974.
Fourteen simple indoor garden projects are described.

Mayer, Mercer. *Frog Goes to Dinner.* Illustrated by the author. New York: Dial Books for Young Readers, 1974.
This wordless picture book shows the adventures of a frog.

———. *One Frog Too Many.* Illustrated by the author. New York: Dial Books for Young Readers, 1975.
This book describes Frog's attempts to rid himself of a new rival—another small frog.

Moore, Eva. *The Cookie Book.* Illustrated by Talivaldis Stubis. New York: Seabury, 1973.
Clear instructions for twelve cookie recipes for special holidays are given in this book.

Oechsli, Helen, and Kelly Oechsli. *In My Garden: A Child's Gardening Book.* Illustrated by Kelly Oechsli. New York: Macmillan, 1985.
This book gives clear instructions for a young gardener to plant a garden, either indoors or outdoors.

Parker, Nancy Winslow. *Working Frog.* New York: Greenwillow Books, 1992.
A bullfrog tells about his life at the Reptile House at the Bronx Zoo.

Paul, Aileen. *Kids Outdoor Gardening.* Illustrated by John DeLulio. New York: Doubleday, 1978.
This book offers tips for beginning young gardeners.

Paul, Aileen, and Arthur Hawkins. *Kids Cooking: The Aileen Paul Cooking School Cookbook.* New York: Doubleday, 1970.
This introduction to cooking gives easy-to-follow recipes and plenty of background information.

Root, Phyllis. *Soup for Supper.* Illustrated by Sue Truesdell. New York: Harper & Row, 1986.
A wee woman tricks a giant into returning the vegetables he has stolen from her garden.

Say, Allen. *A River Dream.* Illustrated by the author. New York: Houghton Mifflin, 1988.
A gift from his uncle, a personal tackle box for fishing supplies, takes Mark on a trip that is part reality and part dream.

Sendak, Maurice. *Where the Wild Things Are.* Illustrated by the author. New York: Harper & Row, 1963. (Caldecott Medal)
This book shows a few moments' wild reverie of an unruly boy who has been sent to his room without supper.

Steig, William. *Brave Irene.* Illustrated by the author. New York: Farrar, Straus & Giroux, 1986.
Little Irene courageously sets out in the midst of a blizzard to deliver a ball gown made by Irene's mother.

Tejima, Keizaburo. *Fox's Dream.* Illustrated by the author. New York: Philomel, 1987.
A fox dreams about the changes the seasons bring and about the birth of a family.

Vincent, Gabrielle. *Ernest and Celestine*. Illustrated by the author. New York: Greenwillow Books, 1982.
A bear, Ernest, consoles his mouse friend when she loses a favorite toy.

Wiesner, David. *Free Fall*. New York: Lothrop, Lee & Shepard, 1988.
A boy's dreams transport him to fantasy lands and adventure far from his bedroom.

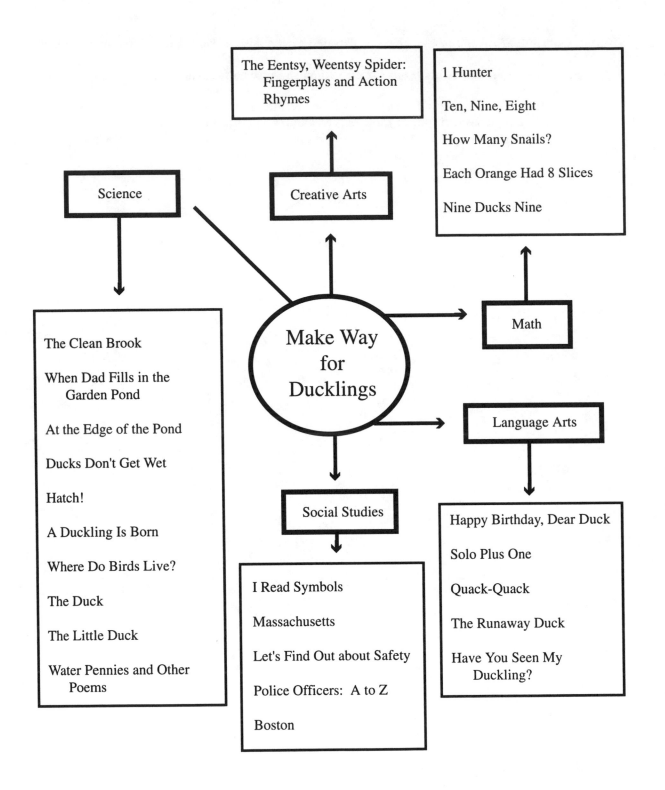

The Eentsy, Weentsy Spider: Fingerplays and Action Rhymes

1 Hunter

Ten, Nine, Eight

How Many Snails?

Each Orange Had 8 Slices

Nine Ducks Nine

Science

Creative Arts

Make Way for Ducklings

Math

The Clean Brook

When Dad Fills in the Garden Pond

At the Edge of the Pond

Ducks Don't Get Wet

Hatch!

A Duckling Is Born

Where Do Birds Live?

The Duck

The Little Duck

Water Pennies and Other Poems

Language Arts

Social Studies

Happy Birthday, Dear Duck

Solo Plus One

Quack-Quack

The Runaway Duck

Have You Seen My Duckling?

I Read Symbols

Massachusetts

Let's Find Out about Safety

Police Officers: A to Z

Boston

13

Make Way for Ducklings
ॐ

McCloskey, Robert. *Make Way for Ducklings*. Illustrated by the author. New York: Viking, 1941. (Caldecott Medal)

Genre: Realistic fiction

Summary: The Mallard family creates a commotion as it searches for a permanent home in Boston.

Content Areas: Language arts, math, science, social studies, and creative arts. This book can be used to introduce a science unit on ducks or a social studies unit on safety.

Brainstorming Starters:

Safety	Ducks
Policeman	Mallards
Boston	Ponds
Public garden	Nests
Beacon Hill	Hatching eggs
Community helpers	Families

Activities for Language Arts

"Shaped Book"

After reading *Make Way for Ducklings* and *The Runaway Duck* aloud to the class, have students prepare booklets. Give them several sheets of paper that have been cut in the shape of a duck. (Use construction paper for the cover and lightweight paper for the inside pages.) On each page, have students draw a picture to represent an event from the story and write one sentence about the picture. Or, have the students read *Happy Birthday, Dear Duck*. Have the students draw a picture to show what they would give a duck for a birthday present and write a description of the present. Other options are writing poems related to the search for a home by Mr. and Mrs. Mallard or about a duckling on a pond.

"My Mother"

Show a number of pictures of baby animals and adult animals. Have volunteers match the babies with the adults. Ask the students what would happen if the mother animals got the babies mixed up. Allow several students to respond. Tell students you are going to read a number of stories about baby animals. Select students who did not participate in the previous discussion and tell them to listen as you read the stories so they can identify what happens to the baby in each story. Read *Solo Plus One*,

Quack-Quack, and *Have You Seen My Duckling?* to the class. After reading the stories, allow the students you selected to tell what happened to each baby and then discuss why the mother was important to the baby in each story. Divide the class into cooperative groups to list things that mother animals do for their babies, such as bring them food or protect them. After each group makes its list, give it the option of developing a picture story about a mother animal and her offspring, drawing pictures and writing a sentence under each picture about the things the students like about their mothers. Each member of the group should contribute to the work. Have each group share its work with the class. Display the finished reports in the classroom.

"Listening"

Ask students if they have ever had a duck for pet. Ask those who have had pet ducks to tell about caring for the duck. Have students who have other pets tell about the care of their pet. Have students make up riddles about caring for pets and share them with the class. For example: "I keep myself clean with my tongue, which is pink. If you don't change my litter it will soon start to stink! What am I?" (Answer: Cat.)

Activities for Math

"Ordinal Numbers"

Use *1 Hunter*; *Ten, Nine, Eight*; *How Many Snails?*; and *Each Orange Had 8 Slices* to introduce ordinal numbers. Prepare a set of duck-shaped word cards with ordinal numbers (first through tenth) on each card, and give ten students the ten cards in random order. Have students line up in the correct order and count off using the ordinal numbers. Have students trade cards and then reorder themselves, using the ordinal numbers. Take the cards and give them to ten other students. Call out numbers at random and have students hold up the card as the number is called.

"Subtraction Ducks"

Have students practice subtraction problems by making picture, word, and number problems. Read *Nine Ducks Nine* to the class. Ask what happened to the total number of ducks as one duck flew away to the rickety bridge on each page. On a flannel board, show nine ducks; remove one and have the students tell how many are left. Continue this activity until there is just one duck left on the flannel board. Divide the class into groups of three to make subtraction booklets by illustrating subtraction problems from nine to one with pictures, words, and numerals. The students can use ducks or other animals to illustrate the problems. One student in the group can draw the pictures (i.e., nine puppy pictures with eight puppies sitting and one puppy walking away), while the second student uses words (i.e., nine puppies - one puppy = eight puppies), and the third student writes the problem using numerals (i.e., 9 - 1 = 8). The three students glue their illustrations of each problem onto one large sheet of drawing paper. This should be repeated for each subtraction problem from 9 - 1 = 8 to 2 - 1 = 1. The eight finished sheets can be fastened together in booklets and shared with the class. Display the booklets on a table.

Activities for Science

"Ecology"

Show pictures of streams, rivers, ponds, and lakes. Select some pictures that clearly reveal dirty water and others that show clean, unpolluted water. Discuss results of pollution on plant and animal life. Read aloud *At the Edge of the Pond*, *Water Pennies and Other Poems*, *The Clean Brook,* and *When Dad Fills in the Garden Pond*. Have students identify what lives in a garden pond. Plan a field trip to a lake, pond, or stream. Have students observe plant and animal life and the condition of the water. Record the students' observations about the water on audiotape. When the class has returned to the classroom, have students draw pictures or write a description of what they observed. When all have completed the activity, discuss the drawings and play the tape recording to recall forgotten facts.

"Ducks"

Display in the science center books showing varieties of ducks and the life cycle of ducks. Have small groups of students go to the center to discuss the pictures and stories found in *The Duck*, *Ducks Don't Get Wet*, *Hatch!*, *A Duckling Is Born*, *The Little Duck*, and *Where Do Birds Live?* Place a list of words, such as *molt, nest, mallard,* and *hatch,* in the science center for definition. Place duck eggs in an incubator and plan what to do when the eggs hatch. Have students project a date for the eggs to hatch. Place a calendar beside the incubator. Each day have a student mark off a day and record any changes. When the ducks hatch, calculate the number of days it took for them to hatch.

Activities for Social Studies

"Developing Map Skills"

After reading *I Read Symbols,* introduce map skills by asking students to draw a map showing the way to school. Explain the symbols N, S, E, and W, as well as top, bottom, legends, and other simple map symbols. Have the students place the symbols on their maps. Plan a neighborhood field trip. Assign students different landmarks to observe. After students observe stores, parks, office buildings, fire hydrants, street signs, and so forth, have them make a giant floor map of the neighborhood on kraft paper. Divide the class into small groups. Show a map of the United States and one of Massachusetts to each small group. Ask the students to find Boston on the maps. Read a book about Boston aloud, having students listen for references to landmarks, such as the Public Garden, Beacon Hill, and the State House. After reading the book aloud, draw a map of Boston that contains symbols for the landmarks identified in the book. Photocopy the map for each student. Divide students into pairs to identify and color each landmark on the map. Good books for this activity are *Massachusetts* and *Boston*.

"Community Helpers"

Introduce the class to the concept of helpers; expand this idea to include community helpers. Show pictures of community helpers, such as policemen, librarians, and the mayor. Allow students to discuss what each community helper does to help the community. List the contribution of each community helper on a chart. Display the pictures with the list. Based on the list, prepare questions that conclude with "Who am I?" for example, "When you're asleep and it starts to snow, I hook up my plow and off I go. Who am I?" (Answer: Snowplow operator.) Have students answer the question by pointing to the correct picture. Allow students to prepare "Who am I?" riddles and read them to the class.

"Safety Rules"

Ask students why they think Mr. and Mrs. Mallard were so careful in selecting a place to build their nest. Read aloud *Let's Find Out About Safety* and *Police Officers: A to Z.* Have students identify the lessons Mr. and Mrs. Mallard taught the ducklings and ask what families and schools teach about safety. Discuss safety rules and list them. Identify ways policemen help keep students and other citizens safe. Invite a policeman to visit the class and discuss safety. After the visit, have students make hand puppets from paper bags to represent the visitor. Expand the list of safety rules by studying rules for boating, swimming, crossing a street, riding a bicycle, skating, petting animals at the zoo, and so forth. Make safety-rule signs from construction paper. Using puppets and signs, have small groups of students role-play safe and unsafe practices of crossing the street, riding bicycles, and swimming.

Activities for Creative Arts

"Duck Mobile"

Divide the class into groups to make mobiles with a mother duck on top and eight little ducks hanging down. Provide two wire hangers and wire or string to tie them together for the frame of the mobile. Provide construction paper, scissors, glue, and crayons to make the little ducks from patterns. The completed mobiles can be displayed in the science center.

"Duck Walk and Sing"

Discuss how ducks walk in a row. Role-play *Make Way for Ducklings* with the students, waddling in a line as the ducklings did. Sing "Six Little Ducks" from the book *The Eentsy, Weentsy Spider: Fingerplays and Action Rhymes.*

Bulletin Boards

"Safety"

After reading *Let's Find Out About Safety* and *Mr. Gumpy's Outing,* have students help plan a bulletin board display. In the center of the bulletin board place a piece of construction paper shaped like a stop sign. On the sign write the phrase *Safety Rules.* Across the top of the bulletin board place pictures of a house, a school, and people crossing a street or riding bicycles. Place a large, ruled sheet of yellow construction paper under each of the three pictures. Divide the class into three groups to cooperatively formulate safety rules for the home, school, and community. After each group decides on five to ten safety rules, write the rules under the appropriate picture.

"Duck Facts"

Bring in wildlife pictures of ducks from magazines. Have students select pictures and hang them on the bulletin board. Have students research facts about ducks from reference materials. Make a pattern of a duck and use it to cut several sheets of paper. Have students write their facts on the duck figures. Place the figures around the pictures of the ducks.

Related Books

Ayres, Pam. *When Dad Fills in the Garden Pond*. Illustrated by Graham Percy. New York: Alfred A. Knopf, 1988.
A garden pond that has served as a home for wildlife is saved.

Bang, Molly. *Ten, Nine, Eight*. Illustrated by the author. New York: Greenwillow Books, 1983. (Caldecott Honor)
A black father and child have a tender bedtime countdown.

Bartlett, Margaret F. *The Clean Brook*. Illustrated by Aldren A. Watson. New York: Thomas Y. Crowell, 1960.
The process of dirtying and purifying a brook is told through the activities of plants and animals.

Bodecher, N. M. *Water Pennies and Other Poems*. Illustrated by Erik Blegvad. New York: Macmillan (Margaret K. McElderry Books), 1991.
Poems about life around freshwater ponds are illustrated in this book.

Bunting, Eve. *Happy Birthday, Dear Duck*. Illustrated by Jan Brett. Boston: Houghton Mifflin (Clarion Books), 1988.
In this read-aloud book, Duck's animal friends give him puzzling presents for his birthday, until the last gift arrives.

Carpenter, Allan. *Massachusetts*. Chicago: Children's Press (The New Enchantment of America Series), 1978.
This information book gives an introduction to the state of Massachusetts.

Cole, Joanna, and Stephanie Calmenson. *The Eentsy, Weentsy Spider: Fingerplays and Action Rhymes*. Illustrated by Alan Tiegreen. New York: Mulberry Books, 1991.
This is a collection of songs and action rhymes intended for use with fingerplays and physical activity.

Dewey, Jennifer Owings. *At the Edge of the Pond*. Illustrated by the author. Waltham, Mass.: Little, Brown, 1987.
Each aspect of pond life is captured by delicate, colored-pencil drawings.

Dunn, Judy. *The Little Duck*. Illustrated by Phoebe Dunn. New York: Random House, 1976.
Pictures are used to depict one year in the life of a duck.

Giganti, Paul Jr. *Each Orange Had 8 Slices*. Illustrated by Donald Crews. New York: Greenwillow Books, 1992.
This is an ordinal counting book that introduces beginning math concepts and reinforces visual literacy.

———. *How Many Snails?* Illustrated by Donald Crews. New York: Greenwillow Books, 1988.
The words and illustrations in this counting book will interest beginning readers.

Golden, Augusta. *Ducks Don't Get Wet*. Illustrated by Leonard Kessler. New York: Thomas Y. Crowell, 1965.
This information book describes an easy experiment that clarifies why ducks can shed water.

Hayes, Susan. *Nine Ducks Nine*. Illustrated by the author. New York: Lothrop, Lee & Shepard, 1990.
This counting book shows subtraction as each duck flies away.

Henley, Karyn. *Hatch*! Illustrated by Susan Kennedy. Minneapolis, Minn.: Carolrhoda Books, 1980.
A variety of nest-making, egg-laying, and hatching methods are described.

Hirschi, Ron. *Where Do Birds Live?* Photographs by Galen Burrell. New York: Walker, 1987.
Readers are introduced to birds' habitats, including ponds, rivers, old trees, mountains, and backyards.

Hoban, Tana. *I Read Symbols*. New York: Greenwillow Books, 1983.
This book introduces the most common traffic signs and signals.

Hutchins, Pat. *1 Hunter*. New York: Mulberry Books, 1982.
As one hunter goes through the forest he is seen by two elephants, three giraffes, four ostriches, and so forth.

Isenbart, Hans-Heinrich. *A Duckling Is Born*. Photographs by Othmar Baumli. New York: Putnam, 1981.
Text and illustrations explain the development of a chick from a tiny spot on the yolk through hatching.

Johnson, Jean. *Police Officers: A to Z*. Illustrated by the author. New York: Walker, 1985.
This gives an excellent introduction to the role of the police officer as community helper and peacekeeper.

Lyon, David. *The Runaway Duck*. Illustrated by the author. New York: Lothrop, Lee & Shepard, 1985.
A toy duck has many adventures.

McCloskey, Robert. *Make Way for Ducklings*. Illustrated by the author. New York: Viking, 1941.
The Mallard Family creates a commotion as it searches for a permanent home in Boston.

Monke, Ingrid. *Boston*. Illustrated with photographs. Minneapolis, Minn.: Dillon, 1988.
An information book that describes the city of Boston, describing neighborhoods, attractions, festivals, and historic sites.

Scamell, Ragnhild. *Solo Plus One*. Illustrated by Elizabeth Martland. Boston: Little, Brown, 1992.
A baby chick adopts an unwilling cat as a parent.

Shapp, Martha, and Charles Shapp. *Let's Find Out About Safety*. Illustrated by Carolyn Bentley. New York: Franklin Watts, 1975.
This book tells about safety at home, at school, and outdoors.

Sheehan, Angela. *The Duck*. Illustrated by Maurice Pledger and Bernard Robinson. New York: Franklin Watts, 1979.
Many basic facts are given in this account, such as eating habits, migration, and natural enemies.

Stehr, Frederic. *Quack-Quack*. Illustrated by the author. New York: Farrar, Straus & Giroux (Sunburst Books), 1988.
A duckling hatches while its mother is away from the nest and assumes that the first animal it sees, a frog, is its mother.

Tafuri, Nancy. *Have You Seen My Duckling?* New York: Greenwillow Books, 1984. (Caldecott Honor)
This is the story of a mother looking for her duckling, who has left the nest and is hiding.

Supplemental Reading

Andersen, Hans Christian. *The Ugly Duckling.* Retold and illustrated by Lorinda B. Cauley. San Diego, Calif.: Harcourt Brace Jovanovich, 1979.
The ugly duckling spends an unhappy year until he grows into a beautiful swan.

Berends, Polly Berrien. *The Case of the Elevator Duck.* Illustrated by James K. Washburn. New York: Random House, 1973.
A funny story about a duck found in a housing project's elevator.

Burningham, John. *Mr. Gumpy's Outing.* New York: Henry Holt, 1971.
Mr. Gumpy takes two children and an assortment of animals for a ride in his boat, and they do not obey safety instructions.

Burstein, Fred. *Whispering in the Park.* Illustrated by Helen Cogancherry. New York: Bradbury Press, 1991.
Miriam and Sophie discover fish in the pond at the park.

Featherly, Jay. *Ko-Hoh: The Call of the Trumpeter Swan.* Photographs by the author. Minneapolis, Minn.: Carolrhoda Books (Nature Watch Books), 1986.
The life cycle, nest building, mating, raising of young, and other behaviors of the trumpeter swan are clearly explained in this book.

Flack, Marjorie. *The Story About Ping.* New York: Viking, 1933.
A little Peking duck is accidentally separated from his family on the Yangtze River.

George, William T. *Box Turtle at Long Pond.* Illustrated by Lindsay Barrett George. New York: Greenwillow Books, 1989.
Box Turtle basks in the sun, searches for food, and escapes a raccoon.

George, William T., and Lindsay Barrett George. *Beaver at Long Pond.* Illustrated by Lindsay Barrett George. New York: Greenwillow Books, 1988.
As animals on the pond are settling down for the night, Beaver is just starting his nightly adventure.

Fantasy

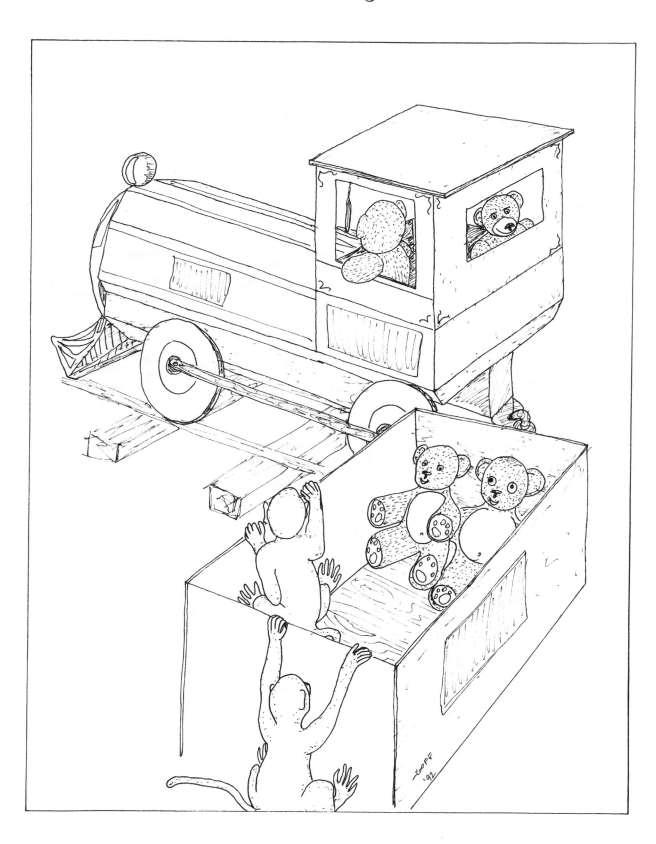

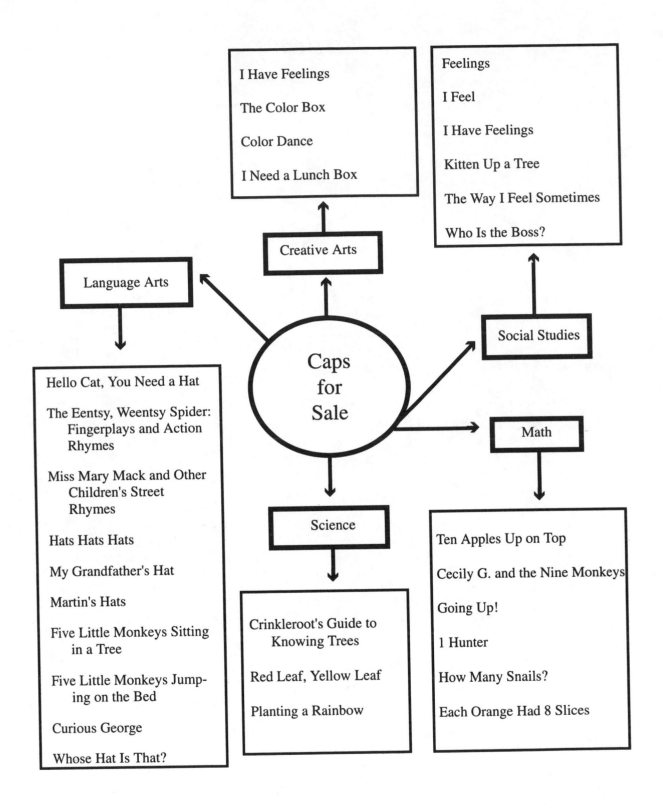

Creative Arts

I Have Feelings

The Color Box

Color Dance

I Need a Lunch Box

Social Studies

Feelings

I Feel

I Have Feelings

Kitten Up a Tree

The Way I Feel Sometimes

Who Is the Boss?

Language Arts

Hello Cat, You Need a Hat

The Eentsy, Weentsy Spider: Fingerplays and Action Rhymes

Miss Mary Mack and Other Children's Street Rhymes

Hats Hats Hats

My Grandfather's Hat

Martin's Hats

Five Little Monkeys Sitting in a Tree

Five Little Monkeys Jumping on the Bed

Curious George

Whose Hat Is That?

Caps for Sale

Math

Ten Apples Up on Top

Cecily G. and the Nine Monkeys

Going Up!

1 Hunter

How Many Snails?

Each Orange Had 8 Slices

Science

Crinkleroot's Guide to Knowing Trees

Red Leaf, Yellow Leaf

Planting a Rainbow

14

Caps for Sale

ৡ

Slobodkina, Esphyr. *Caps for Sale: A Tale of a Peddler, Some Monkeys and Their Monkey Business*. Illustrated by the author. Reading, Mass: Addison-Wesley, 1947.

Genre: Animal story—fantasy

Summary: A routine day for a cap salesman takes an unusual turn when a monkey climbs into a tree with his wares.

Content Areas: Language arts, math, science, social studies, and creative arts. This book can be used to introduce a social studies unit on feelings, a language arts unit on visual and color discrimination and word refrains, or a math unit to review addition and subtraction.

Brainstorming Starters:

Monkey	Blue
Peddler	Brown
Wares	Checked
Caps	Angry
Colors	For sale
Gray	Trees
Red	

Activities for Language Arts

"Word Refrain"

Read the books *Caps for Sale*; *Five Little Monkeys Sitting in a Tree*; *Five Little Monkeys Jumping on the Bed*; and *Hello Cat, You Need a Hat* to the class, encouraging students to repeat refrains as the story is read. Small groups can develop new refrains, for example, "Shoes! Shoes for sale!" and "You monkeys, you! You must give back my shoes!" Have each small group present the refrains and the rest of the class echo them. Other books that would be helpful are *The Eentsy, Weentsy Spider: Fingerplays and Action Rhymes* and *Miss Mary Mack and Other Children's Street Rhymes*.

"Visual and Color Discrimination"

Read *Curious George* and discuss the hat George wears. Draw six different caps (a policeman, Boy Scout, fireman, baseball player, nurse, bicycle rider, or others) on a piece of construction paper that has been divided into six equal squares. Copy these on two red, two blue, two green, two yellow, two tan, and two gray sheets of construction paper. Mount the sheets of construction paper on tagboard, laminate the sheets, and then cut them apart to form cards. Shuffle the cards and place them in a stack on a table with different kinds of hats and caps. Allow two students to shuffle the cards and place them face down on the table, then attempt to locate two cards that match. Each student keeps the pairs that he or she finds. When all the matches have been made, have the students shuffle the card and sort them by colors. Students can discuss the differences in the hats and identify who would wear each one.

"Puppets"

Place construction paper, paper bags, sticks, and sock puppets on a table. Divide students into cooperative groups to develop a story about a monkey and an item, such as a cap. Then have them make puppets and other props and present the story to the class.

"Writing Activity"

Each student can design a cap, write a description of it, and try to sell the cap to a group of classmates. Have each group pick one cap to try to sell to the entire class. Following the selection of the winning design, class members can look at all of the caps and select the largest, most colorful, or best of its kind. Books available for this activity are *Hats Hats Hats*; *My Grandfather's Hat*; *Martin's Hats*; *Hello Cat, You Need a Hat*; or *Whose Hat Is That?*

Activities for Math

"Addition and Subtraction"

Using construction paper or tagboard, make a number of monkeys and a number of caps that can be placed on the monkeys (see page 129). Write an addition or subtraction problem on each monkey and an answer on each cap. Also write the answers on the back of the monkey for self-checking. Students can work alone or in pairs to match the correct cap with each monkey. After all caps have been placed on the monkeys, have students turn each monkey over to see if the correct match was made. The books *1 Hunter* and *How Many Snails?* help students write numbers from one to ten.

"Ordering"

On a card, draw a peddler with one cap on his head; on a second card draw a second peddler with two caps on his head; repeat until you have ten peddlers, the last with ten caps on his head. This is one set of peddlers. Copy the set several times. Divide the class into small groups of two to four students each. Give each group a set of cards. Have students take turns placing the pictures in order from the peddler with the smallest number of caps to the peddler with the largest number of caps. Students can compare their work. *Each Orange Had 8 Slices*, *Cecily G. and the Nine Monkeys*, *Going Up!*, and *Ten Apples Up on Top* would reinforce ordering activities.

Activities for Science

"Trees"

Read *Crinkleroot's Guide to Knowing Trees.* Show students pictures of different kinds of trees. Introduce the vocabulary terms *trunk, branch, bark, leaves,* and *fruit.* Label and display pieces of bark, branches, leaves, and fruit from various trees. Working in small groups, have the students identify the differences in the bark, branches, leaves, and fruit. Allow students to identify animals that climb or live in trees and draw a picture of a tree with animals on the branches. Allow each student to tell about the drawing. Other books available for this activity are *Red Leaf, Yellow Leaf* and *Planting a Rainbow.*

Activities for Social Studies

"Feelings"

Caps for Sale; Feelings; I Feel: I Have Feelings; Kitten Up a Tree; The Way I Feel Sometimes; and *Who Is the Boss?* can be used to introduce feelings. Display a number of pictures that express a variety of feelings. Use a chart to display the name of each feeling. Form groups to represent various feelings, such as happy, sad, or mad. Give each group a mirror so that students can see themselves as they make faces to represent the assigned feeling. After the groups decide which student's expression best represents the feeling, have those students make the face for the class. Have students respond to a story starter, such as "When I am angry, I. . . ."

"Follow the Monkey"

In this activity, a student leads the class in making "monkey faces" from the feelings that have been studied. Select a student to be the "monkey." After selecting a picture that was placed face down on a table, the child who is the "monkey" makes a face to represent the feeling in the picture. The class copies the "monkey's" face, and the "monkey" selects the best one. The selected child becomes the "monkey," and the game continues until several children have had the opportunity to be the leader.

Activities for Creative Arts

"Finger Painting to Music"

Read the book *I Have Feelings.* Have students finger paint to different kinds of music that express various feelings. Have students select the color of paint that represents the feeling the music expresses. Label each painting as students complete the activity.

"Caps"

Have students design caps on tagboard; use scraps of materials, yarn, wallpaper, sequins, and bells to decorate the caps. When this is completed, stage a parade in which students display the caps.

"Counting Colors Big Book"

Divide the class into eleven groups to construct a counting big book of selected colors. Books that would help students with colors are: *The Color Box, Color Dance,* and *I Need a Lunch Box.* Assign one group to make the cover. Assign each of the remaining ten groups one color and a number from one to ten. Provide each group with crayons, tempera paint, markers, glue, various colors of tissue paper and construction paper, and an eighteen-by-twenty four-inch sheet of white paper or tagboard. If the group has been assigned the color blue and the number three, the assignment is to draw three caps on the sheet, color each one in some shade of blue, and write the numeral three and the phrase "three blue caps" in blue on that page. If the assigned number is seven and the color is purple, the seven caps would be purple and the numeral and sentence would be written in a matching color. When all group work has been completed, laminate the pages and place them in correct order before fastening the work together with four plastic rings. Have the students share the book in small groups and display it in the library center.

Bulletin Boards

"Caps"
In the center of the bulletin board place the heading *How Many Hats?* Take a picture of each student wearing a hat selected from several hats (i.e., nurse, fireman, policeman, football) that have been displayed and discussed. Mount each picture on construction paper. Place the pictures on the branches of a tree that has been tacked to the bulletin board. Place several monkeys made from heavy tagboard under the branches. Each monkey holds a question, such as "How many students are wearing a nurse's cap?" or "Which hat did the most students select?" Have students use the book *Whose Hat Is That?* in this activity.

"Caps for Sale"
Label the bulletin board with the heading *Caps for Sale.* Display the hats from the creative arts activity "Caps" on a bulletin board. Assign a value of five, ten, or twenty-five cents to each cap, and write the price under each cap. Affix two large envelopes to the bottom of the board containing addition and subtraction problems. Students can select a problem card and attempt to solve the problem. Students can work in pairs, with one student solving the problem and the other student verifying the answer. The questions might include "You have seventy-five cents to buy one hat. How many choices do you have?" or "How many caps cost less than fifty cents?"

Related Books

Aliki. *Feelings*. Illustrated by the author. New York: Mulberry Books, 1984.
A range of emotions are displayed in this book.

Ancona, George. *I Feel*. New York: E. P. Dutton, 1977.
Through photographs, this book explores the expressions on a person's face.

Arnosky, Jim. *Crinkleroot's Guide to Knowing Trees*. New York: Macmillan (Bradbury Press), 1992.
This information book can be used to identify trees by their leaves, stems, and seeds.

Berger, Terry. *I Have Feelings*. Photographs by I. Howard Spivak. New York: Behavioral, 1971.
Text and photos reveal various feelings experienced by children, showing them that their feelings are natural.

Blos, Joan W. *Martin's Hats*. Illustrated by Marc Simont. New York: William Morrow, 1984.
A colorful book portrays the adventures of Martin wearing hats.

Caines, Jeannette. *I Need a Lunch Box*. Illustrated by Pat Cummings. New York: Harper & Row, 1988.
This picture book about a young African American boy emphasizes colors, days of the week, and a young child's imagination.

Christelow, Eileen. *Five Little Monkeys Jumping on the Bed*. New York: Houghton Mifflin (Clarion Books), 1991.
A predictable story about five monkeys jumping on the bed when it is time for bed.

————. *Five Little Monkeys Sitting in a Tree*. New York: Houghton Mifflin (Clarion Books), 1991.
Five monkeys delight in teasing a crocodile.

Cole, Joanna, and Stephanie Calmenson. *The Eentsy, Weentsy Spider: Fingerplays and Action Rhymes*. Illustrated by Alan Tiegreen. New York: Mulberry Books, 1991.
A collection of songs and action rhymes intended for use with fingerplays and physical activity.

————. *Miss Mary Mack and Other Children's Street Rhymes*. Illustrated by Alan Tiegreen. New York: Morrow Junior Books, 1990.
Contains a number of street rhymes for ball bouncing, counting out, and hand clapping.

de Regniers, Beatrice. *The Way I Feel Sometimes*. Illustrated by Susan Meddaugh. New York: Houghton Mifflin (Clarion Books), 1991.
This book of poems appeals to the various emotions of children.

Dodds, Dayle Ann. *The Color Box*. Illustrated by Giles Laroche. Boston: Little, Brown, 1992.
A monkey climbs into a box and discovers a world of color.

Ehlert, Lois. *Planting a Rainbow*. Illustrated by the author. New York: Harcourt Brace Jovanovich, 1988.
Colors are introduced through a family garden.

————. *Red Leaf, Yellow Leaf*. New York: Harcourt Brace Jovanovich, 1991.
This information book describes the growth cycle of a tree.

Gelman, Rita. *Hello Cat, You Need a Hat.* Illustrated by Eric Gurney. New York: Scholastic, 1991.
In this book of rhyming words, a cat is encouraged to wear a hat.

Giganti, Paul Jr. *Each Orange Had 8 Slices.* Illustrated by Donald Crews. New York: Greenwillow Books, 1992.
An ordinal counting book that introduces beginning math concepts and reinforces visual literacy.

————. *How Many Snails?* Illustrated by Donald Crews. New York: Greenwillow Books, 1988.
The words and illustrations in this counting book will interest beginning readers.

Goffin, Josse. *Who Is the Boss?* Illustrated by the author. New York: Houghton Mifflin (Clarion Books), 1992.
Two men in bowler caps while sailing argue about many things before crashing into an iceberg.

Hutchins, Pat. *1 Hunter.* New York: Mulberry Books, 1982.
As a hunter goes through the forest he is seen by two elephants, three giraffes, four ostriches, etc.

Jonas, Ann. *Color Dance.* New York: Greenwillow Books, 1989.
This concept book introduces color combinations through dances.

Kanao, Keiko. *Kitten Up a Tree.* New York: Alfred A. Knopf, 1987.
A young kitten desires to fly and must be rescued from a tree.

LeSieg, Theo. *Ten Apples Up on Top.* Illustrated by Roy McKie. New York: Random House, 1961.
A counting book about animals carrying apples on their heads.

Morris, Ann. *Hats Hats Hats.* Photographs by Ken Heyman. New York: Lothrop, Lee & Shepard, 1989.
This book shows all kinds of hats—soft, hard, snugly, and hooded.

Rey, H. A. *Cecily G. and the Nine Monkeys.* New York: Houghton Mifflin, 1942.
The book tells the story of a lonely giraffe and nine monkeys with no home.

————. *Curious George.* New York: Houghton Mifflin, 1941.
The adventures of George and the man in the yellow hat begin in this book.

Roy, Ron. *Whose Hat Is That?* Illustrated by Rosemarie Hausherr. New York: Houghton Mifflin (Clarion Books), 1991.
Photographs show children and adults wearing different kinds of hats.

Scheller, Melanie. *My Grandfather's Hat.* Illustrated by Keiko Narahashi. New York: Margaret K. McElderry Books, 1992.
Jason reshapes his grandfather's hat after he jumps on it.

Sis, Peter. *Going Up!* New York: Greenwillow Books, 1989.
The story provides information on colors and ordinal numbers.

Slobodkina, Esphyr. *Caps for Sale: A Tale of a Peddler, Some Monkeys and Their Monkey Business.* Illustrated by the author. Reading, Mass.: Addison-Wesley, 1947.
A routine day for a cap salesman takes an unusual turn when a monkey climbs into a tree with his wares.

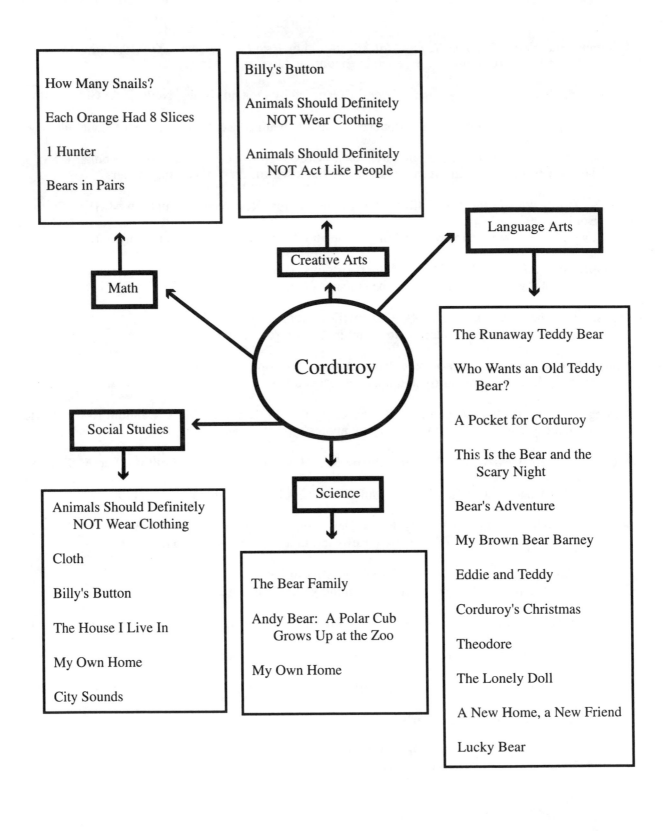

How Many Snails?

Each Orange Had 8 Slices

1 Hunter

Bears in Pairs

Billy's Button

Animals Should Definitely NOT Wear Clothing

Animals Should Definitely NOT Act Like People

Language Arts

Creative Arts

Math

Corduroy

The Runaway Teddy Bear

Who Wants an Old Teddy Bear?

A Pocket for Corduroy

This Is the Bear and the Scary Night

Bear's Adventure

My Brown Bear Barney

Eddie and Teddy

Corduroy's Christmas

Theodore

The Lonely Doll

A New Home, a New Friend

Lucky Bear

Social Studies

Science

Animals Should Definitely NOT Wear Clothing

Cloth

Billy's Button

The House I Live In

My Own Home

City Sounds

The Bear Family

Andy Bear: A Polar Cub Grows Up at the Zoo

My Own Home

15

Corduroy

ॐ

Freeman, Don. *Corduroy*. Illustrated by the author. New York: Viking Penguin, 1968.

Genre: Fantasy

Summary: A teddy bear with a missing button on his coveralls seems destined for a lonely life in a department store until he meets a little girl, Lisa. Lisa uses the savings in her piggy bank to give Corduroy a new home.

Content Areas: Language arts, math, science, social studies, and creative arts. This book can be used in social studies to introduce a unit on kinds of stores and homes and in language arts for description and vocabulary expansion.

Brainstorming Starters:

Teddy bear	Escalator
Overalls	Upstairs
Buttons	Furniture
Straps	Home
Piggy bank	Palace
Department store	Apartment
Customer	Mountain
Shopper	Enormous
Watchman	Small

Activities for Language Arts

"Poems"

After reading *Corduroy*, *Corduroy's Christmas*, *Lucky Bear*, *The Lonely Doll*, *The Runaway Teddy Bear*, or *Who Wants an Old Teddy Bear?*, have students talk about a favorite stuffed animal or toy and think about how they obtained the animal or toy. Invite them to bring the stuffed animal to class for show and tell the next day. Students can draw a picture of the chosen toy or animal and write a poem about the toy below its picture. Display the pictures and poems on the bulletin board.

"Tone of Voice"

Discuss the use of soft and loud voices in different places, such as the playground, the library, a football game, or at home playing with toys. Allow several students to demonstrate the volume of their voices and tell why each is appropriate or inappropriate for the classroom. In small groups, have students practice using soft voices by describing a favorite stuffed animal to the student sitting in the next desk or space. Then have students speak loudly to make an announcement or other public speech.

"Adventures for Corduroy"

After reading *Eddie and Teddy*, *A Pocket for Corduroy*, *Theodore*, *This Is the Bear and the Scary Night*, or *Bear's Adventure*, divide students into groups to plan new adventures for Corduroy or another bear. In each group, have students draw a picture and write a sentence about the new adventure; have them combine their pictures to form books. Place the books in the library center.

"No Place Like Home"

After discussing how Corduroy wanted a home and his feelings after finding one, have students list on the chalkboard two or three nice things about having a home. Write a story starter "There is no place like home. . ." on the board. Have students complete this story starter and share with the class. Read *My Brown Bear Barney* or *A New Home, a New Friend*.

Activities for Math

"Counting Bears"

Make fifty three-by-five-inch cards with an identical bear on each card. Number ten of the cards one through ten. Write the numeral below the bear on each card. On ten additional cards, glue a corresponding number of cardboard buttons. On the remainder of the cards, write addition and subtraction problems for which the answer is ten or less. Laminate all of the cards to make them more durable. The cards can be used for matching numbers and buttons, putting in numerical order, and problem-solving. Books that help students learn numbers are *Bears in Pairs*, *How Many Snails?*, *Each Orange Had 8 Slices*, and *1 Hunter*.

"Button Sorting"

This is an activity for groups of five students. For each student in the group, place ten buttons that are different in color and size in a clear sandwich bag, along with a set of instructions for sorting the buttons by color, size, shape, or ascending or descending number. Students take turns reading the instructions in their bags, and all students in the group follow each instruction. Additional instructions could include, "Sort the buttons by placing the smallest button first and the largest button last in a line"; "Place the buttons in a row in this order: blue, green, red, black, and orange"; or "Sort by placing the round ones first, the square ones in the middle, and other shapes last." Students can compare their work.

Activities for Science

"Bears"

Look at pictures of various kinds of bears and read *The Bear Family* and *Andy Bear: A Polar Cub Grows Up at the Zoo*. Find out facts about bears from books and other resources. Give students bears cut from construction paper or tagboard. Have each student record a fact about bears on the paper bear and hang it on the bulletin board.

"Animal Homes"

Read *My Own Home* and discuss what the young owl was looking for. Ask students what kinds of homes various animals live in. List their answers on the board. Show the class pictures of various animals and pictures of their homes, such as birds and nests, whales and oceans, apes and jungles, bats and caves, bees and hives, scorpions and deserts, big horn sheep and mountains, and so forth. As students look at the pictures, ask them what happens to animals when they are moved from their natural homes, as when a killer whale like Shamu is moved to a marine park like Sea World. Then ask them what might happen if the climate changes or their food supply is no longer available, for example, what happened to the woolly mammoth after the Ice Age or what happens to deer in a hard winter. After discussing these problems and arriving at the idea of extinction, have volunteers match pictures of animals with pictures of their homes. Using trade books and pictures, help students clear up any confusion about where the animals live. Divide the class into collaborative groups to research several of the pictured animals, their habitats, and whether they are on an endangered species list. After research, have the students tell the class how and why each animal's habitat suits specific characteristics of that animal, for example, how rivers (not lakes) suit the spawning habits of salmon. Have each group report its findings to the class and write the names of endangered animals on a chart to be displayed in the school hallway.

Activities for Social Studies

"Fabrics"

After reading *Corduroy, Animals Should Definitely NOT Wear Clothing, Cloth,* and *Billy's Button*, discuss fabrics from which clothes are made. On the science table, display samples of cotton, rayon, silk, wool, corduroy, burlap, and other fabrics. Have pairs of students feel the materials and describe them using terms such as rough, smooth, soft, or hard. Have the students name what piece of clothing could be made from each fabric. Have them select one fabric and describe it in a journal entry.

"Field Trip"

Visit a department store. Talk to a salesperson and a security guard about their jobs and the hours they work. Using a tape recorder, record the conversation. After returning to school, listen to the tape. Give students the option of drawing a picture or writing a sentence or two to explain what they would do if they were a salesperson or security guard who discovered a toy bear walking up the escalator.

"Houses"

Show a picture of one class member's house, and ask who lives in the house. Read the books *The House I Live In, My Own Home,* and *City Sounds,* and display pictures of different kinds of homes, such as nests, tents, castles, doghouses, duplexes, tree houses, apartment houses, trailers, and the White House. Have students identify who or what might live in each house. Have each student select a house (apartment house, trailer, cottage) cut from construction paper and record his or her home address on the house. If a child does not know the address, provide the information. While the students are completing this activity, display building materials for houses, such as bricks, wood, nails, and tiles. Discuss them. Provide samples of paints and wallpaper. Divide students into cooperative groups to construct a village from small cardboard boxes of different sizes and shapes. Give each group one box. Each group may decide on the type house to be built, the number of windows and doors it will have, and whether it will have porches, decks, and other features. Provide cardboard, tape, paint, glue, craft sticks, and paper for students to construct the house designed by the group.

Activities for Creative Arts

"Button Collage"

After reading *Billy's Button*, students may enjoy creating a collage using buttons. In the art center, provide the materials for the collage, including many buttons of various sizes and colors, sturdy paper plates, round cardboard (pizza parlor), glue, scissors, tape, pieces of yarn, and scraps of many kinds of fabrics. Have students select a paper plate or round cardboard and enough materials to create a collage that illustrates a number, a letter, or a picture from *Billy's Button* or *Corduroy*. Use completed collages as a border for the bulletin board.

"Dress the Bears"

After sharing *Animals Should Definitely NOT Wear Clothing* and *Animals Should Definitely NOT Act Like People*, students can dress a bear. Give each student a piece of tagboard with a simple drawing of a bear character. In the art center, provide scraps of materials (i.e., corduroy, wool, burlap, silk, or cotton), a variety of buttons, glue, scissors, tape, needles, thread, and yarn. Display the dressed bears on the bulletin board.

Bulletin Boards

"Bear Facts"

Form a border around the bulletin board using the button collages the students made in the creative arts activity "Button Collage." Using letter cut from fabric, write the words *Bear Facts* in the center of the bulletin board. Have students place the tagboard bears containing information about bears (from the science activity "Bears") on the bulletin board.

"Picture Poems"

Encourage students to bring a stuffed toy to use during the language arts activity "Poems." Take pictures of small groups of students with their stuffed toys. Place the pictures on the bulletin board under the heading *Corduroy's New Friends*. The students' picture poems may be placed around the heading or around the edges of the board.

Related Books

Accorsi, William. *Billy's Button*. New York: Greenwillow Books, 1992.
A button game for the whole family.

Barrett, Judi. *Animals Should Definitely NOT Act Like People*. Illustrated by Ron Barrett. New York: Scholastic, 1992.
This picture story book reveals why animals should act like animals.

———. *Animals Should Definitely NOT Wear Clothing*. Illustrated by Ron Barrett. New York: Scholastic, 1992.
This picture story book reveals why bears should not wear clothes like people.

Betz, Dieter. *The Bear Family*. New York: William Morrow (Tambourine), 1992.
Photographs show the life of Alaskan bears.

Blathwayt, Benedict. *Bear's Adventure*. New York: Alfred A. Knopf, 1988.
A teddy bear has a wild sea adventure after being left on the beach.

Butler, Dorothy. *My Brown Bear Barney*. Illustrated by Elizabeth Fuller. New York: William Morrow (Greenwillow Books), 1989.
A little girl plans to take her teddy bear to school after her mother declared he must stay at home.

Clarke, Gus. *Eddie and Teddy*. New York: William Morrow (Mulberry Books), 1992.
When Eddie goes to school, his teddy bear goes too.

Emberley, Rebecca. *City Sounds*. New York: Scholastic, 1992.
Scenes and sounds of a city are revealed in this book.

Freeman, Don. *Corduroy*. Illustrated by the author. New York: Viking Penguin, 1968.
A teddy bear with a missing button on his coveralls seems destined for a lonely life in a department store until he meets a little girl, Lisa. Lisa uses the savings in her piggy bank to give Corduroy a new home.

———. *A Pocket for Corduroy*. New York: Viking, 1978.
This book tells the story of Corduroy's desire for a pocket.

Giganti, Paul Jr. *Each Orange Had 8 Slices*. Illustrated by Donald Crews. New York: Greenwillow Books, 1992.
This is an ordinal counting book that introduces beginning math concepts and reinforces visual literacy.

———. *How Many Snails?* Illustrated by Donald Crews. New York: Greenwillow Books, 1988.
The words and illustrations in this counting book will interest beginning readers.

Hayes, Sarah. *This Is the Bear and the Scary Night*. Illustrated by Helen Craig. Boston: Little, Brown (Joy Street Books), 1992.
A boy leaves a lovable stuffed bear on a park bench, and the bear has an adventure.

Hennessy, B. G. *Corduroy's Christmas*. Illustrated by Lisa McCue. New York: Viking, 1992.
    Corduroy experiences Christmas with a tree and presents.

Hofmann, Ginnie. *The Runaway Teddy Bear*. New York: Random House, 1986.
    Arthur the teddy bear finds out that there is no place like home.

———. *Who Wants an Old Teddy Bear?* New York: Random House, 1980.
    This story portrays the love between a very small boy and a teddy bear.

Hoopes, Lyn L. *My Own Home*. New York: Harcourt Brace Jovanovich, 1991.
    A young owl tries to find out the meaning of home.

Hutchins, Pat. *1 Hunter*. New York: Mulberry Books, 1982.
    As one hunter goes through the forest he is seen by two elephants, three giraffes, four ostriches, and so forth.

Johnston, Ginny, and Judy Cutchins. *Andy Bear: A Polar Cub Grows Up at the Zoo*. Photographs by Constance Noble. New York: William Morrow, 1985.
    An information book about the first year in the life of a polar bear born at the Atlanta, Georgia, zoo.

Knox, Albert. *Cloth*. Illustrated with photographs. New York: Franklin Watts, 1976.
    An information book that describes types of cloth, their source, and how they are made.

Ormondroyd, Edward. *Theodore*. Illustrated by John Larrecq. New York: Houghton Mifflin, 1966.
    In this adventure story, a teddy bear discovers that being dirty has advantages.

Phillips, Joan. *Lucky Bear*. Illustrated by J. P. Miller. New York: Random House, 1986.
    A teddy bear finds the love of a child.

Seltzer, Isadore. *The House I Live In: At Home in America*. Illustrated by the author. New York: Macmillan, 1992.
    Children are pictured in twelve different houses across the United States.

Wilhelm, Hans. *A New Home, a New Friend*. New York: Random House, 1985.
    A boy adapts to a new home with the help of an abandoned dog.

Wright, Dare. *The Lonely Doll*. Illustrated by the author. Garden City, N.Y.: Doubleday, 1957.
    A doll is no longer lonely after meeting two teddy bears.

Yektai, Niki. *Bears in Pairs*. Illustrated by Diane DeGroat. New York: Macmillan, 1991.
    This is a beginning reader's rhyming book about pairs of bears on their way to a party.

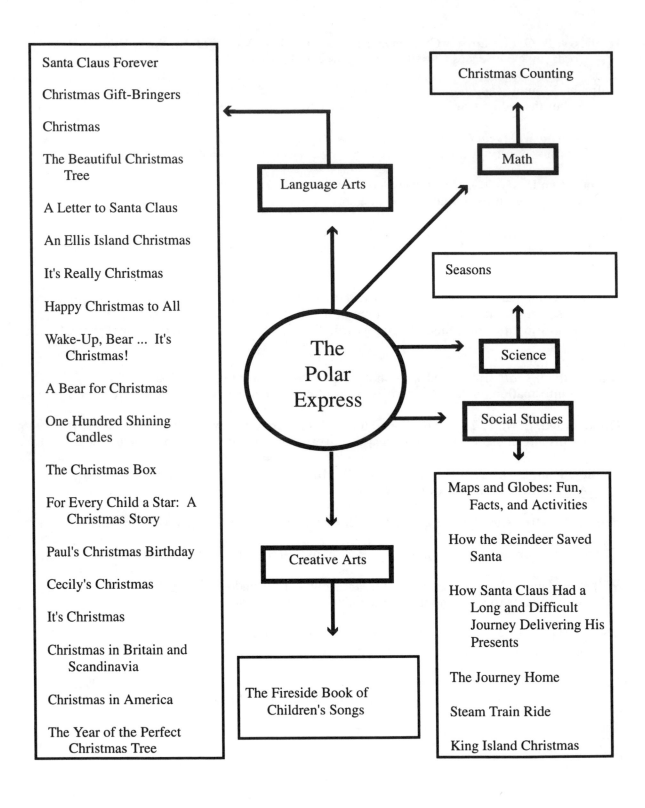

Santa Claus Forever

Christmas Gift-Bringers

Christmas

The Beautiful Christmas
Tree

A Letter to Santa Claus

An Ellis Island Christmas

It's Really Christmas

Happy Christmas to All

Wake-Up, Bear ... It's
Christmas!

A Bear for Christmas

One Hundred Shining
Candles

The Christmas Box

For Every Child a Star: A
Christmas Story

Paul's Christmas Birthday

Cecily's Christmas

It's Christmas

Christmas in Britain and
Scandinavia

Christmas in America

The Year of the Perfect
Christmas Tree

Language Arts

The
Polar
Express

Creative Arts

The Fireside Book of
Children's Songs

Christmas Counting

Math

Seasons

Science

Social Studies

Maps and Globes: Fun,
Facts, and Activities

How the Reindeer Saved
Santa

How Santa Claus Had a
Long and Difficult
Journey Delivering His
Presents

The Journey Home

Steam Train Ride

King Island Christmas

16

The Polar Express

Van Allsburg, Chris. *The Polar Express*. Illustrated by the author. Boston: Houghton Mifflin, 1985. (Caldecott Medal)

Genre: Picture book

Summary: On Christmas Eve, a young boy takes a magical train ride to the North Pole, where he receives the first gift of Christmas.

Content Areas: Language arts, math, science, social studies, and creative arts. This book can be used to bridge the passage between real and make believe. It can be used to introduce a unit on Christmas and Christmas traditions.

Brainstorming Starters:

"True" believer	Christmas
Magical	Snowflakes
North Pole	Wilderness
Polar	Valleys
Traditions	Mountains
Family traditions	Ocean liner
Ringing bells	Train
Elves	Conductor
Gifts	Reindeer
Santa's sleigh	Harness
Holiday	Midnight
Christmas Eve	Sound

Activities for Language Arts

"Christmas Memories"

Read *Santa Claus Forever, Christmas Gift-Bringers, Christmas, Cecily's Christmas, It's Christmas,* or *The Beautiful Christmas Tree*. Introduce the vocabulary terms *memories* and *traditions* by writing them on the board and discussing them. Share with the class one of your childhood Christmas memories. Divide students into groups to share memories, and have several volunteers share their memories with the class. Invite an adult volunteer or guest to discuss the celebration of holidays when he or she was young. Have the class identify several traditions; list them on the board. Have students discuss how activities become traditions. Allow the students to form pairs to draw a picture and write about a Christmas memory or one of the traditions listed on the board. The products can be placed in a booklet entitled *Christmas Memories*.

"Christmas Planning"

Provide each child with a Christmas tree-shaped booklet containing blank pages. Have them construct picture books portraying how Christmas is celebrated by their families. Allow the students to share their booklets and discuss plans for the holiday. Place the following books in the reading center: *The Year of the Perfect Christmas Tree*; *A Letter to Santa Claus*; *An Ellis Island Christmas*; *It's Really Christmas*; *Happy Christmas to All*; *Wake Up, Bear . . . It's Christmas!*; *Christmas in Britain and Scandinavia*; *Christmas in America*; and *A Bear for Christmas*. Encourage students to read several of these books as plans are made for journal writing. Provide topics to guide the writing and follow-up activities each day. For example, one topic might be Christmas meals. Instruct students to write about holiday foods in their journals and then make a recipe book for the holiday. After discussing giving and receiving Christmas cards, have students write a journal entry about a person to whom they would send a Christmas card. A follow-up activity would be to go to the art center and design a Christmas card with a message. Provide envelopes or help students make envelopes that can be addressed, stamped, and placed in the school office to be mailed. Another journal entry can be to make a Christmas wish list to send to Santa. Following this journal entry, have students go to the art center and design a thank-you note to Santa for a past Christmas present. Place these on the class Christmas tree. Another writing exercise is to write a Christmas poem as a journal entry. Students who do not celebrate Christmas could write journal entries and complete activities about the commercial aspects of Christmas or about another holiday, such as Chanukah.

"First Gift of Christmas"

Before reading *The Polar Express*, suggest students read such books as *A Bear for Christmas*, *One Hundred Shining Candles*, *The Christmas Box*, *For Every Child a Star: A Christmas Story*, or *Paul's Christmas Birthday* when thinking about Christmas gifts. After reading *The Polar Express*, discuss why the boy chose the bell when he was told he could select anything from Santa's workshop. Allow students to suggest reasons for the boy's selection and list them on a chalkboard. Give each student a blank sheet of white construction paper. Ask them to respond to the story starter, "If Santa had selected me, the gift I would select would be. . . ." After completing the story, have students illustrate it. Have each student mount the picture on a piece of Christmas wrapping paper that measures one inch larger than the construction paper. The pictures and stories can be placed on the bulletin board.

Activities for Math

"Midnight or 12:00 P.M."

Read *The Polar Express* and point out the sentence about the clock striking midnight. Display a clock with movable hands, and on large cards write *midnight*, *noon*, *a.m.*, *p.m.*, *minute*, *hour*, *clock*, and *12:00*. Discuss the terms and how to differentiate between noon and midnight. Distribute two five-by-seven-inch cards to each student. Have the students write *a.m.* on one side and *p.m.* on the other side of one card and *midnight* and *noon* on opposite sides of the other card. Ask "If the moon and stars are out, is it noon or midnight?" "When you come to school, is it 8:00 a.m. or 8:00 p.m.?" "Is the middle of the day noon or midnight?" and "Is it a.m. or p.m. when you wake up in the morning?" Have students hold up the card with the correct response. When it appears that all of the students are responding correctly, divide the class into groups to develop a list of activities that are done in the a.m., in the p.m., at noon, or at midnight. Compile the lists and share them with the class.

"How Many Bells?"

After reading *The Polar Express* and *Christmas Counting*, fill a one-quart glass jar with small bells. On a table place the jar, slips of paper, and a decorated jar with a slot cut in the lid. During the day, have students estimate the number of bells in the jar, write their estimates on slips of paper, and drop the slips in the other jar. Write each child's estimate on a chart, ranging from the smallest to the largest number. Count the bells, and compare the actual number to the estimates. Divide the class into several groups. Give each group approximately fifty large bells, fifty small bells, and two large baby-food jars. Have each group write an estimate of how many of each size of bell will fit in each jar. To check their estimates, have the students fill the jars and count the bells in each. The students in each group may compare their estimates. Each student who correctly guesses the number will be allowed to select a prize from a "Reward Box," or each child might be given a sticker with "Good work," "Excellent," or Winner" to wear. Ask students what other times or for what other purposes estimates can be used.

Activities for Science

"A Trip to the North Pole"

Look at *Seasons*. Extend the social studies "Travel Poster" activity by planning what clothing to take on a trip to the North Pole. Ask the class to think about the types of clothing that would be needed at the North Pole. Using charts or on an overhead projector, present the class with information about the normal temperatures, amounts of precipitation, wind direction and speed, and the hours of light and darkness at the North Pole. Make frost to show what happens as temperatures change. To make frost, fill a metal can with alternating layers of rock salt, ice, and a little water. Students can observe the outside of the metal can to watch the frost develop. Divide the class into groups for planning clothing to take on the trip. As groups develop the list of clothing, allow students to view the results of the frost experiment and discuss how it was produced. Have each group complete a list of essential clothing for the trip and write the list on a poster shaped like a suitcase. Allow each group to justify the items on the list when presenting it to the class.

"Melting Time"

As an extension of the math activity "Midnight or 12:00 P.M." and the reading of *Seasons*, discuss estimating time. Also discuss how sunshine and shade influence melting time. Freeze two half-gallon milk cartons full of water. Have students estimate how long it will take for the ice to melt. Put one block of ice in the sun and one in the shade. Ask students if they want to revise their estimates. Make a chart showing the estimates of melting time for the two blocks of ice. As each block melts, record how much of each has melted every half hour. Compare the melting time of the blocks of ice, and determine which students were correct in the estimates.

Activities for Social Studies

"Globe"

Display a globe, large map, a bell, *Maps and Globes: Fun, Facts, and Activities*, and *The Polar Express* on a table. Before reading *The Polar Express*, discuss how each of the items are related. Discuss the difference between a globe and a map. Have students find various locations on each.

During the discussion, have seven students hold cards on which *North*, *South*, *East*, *West*, *Continent*, *North Pole*, or *South Pole* are printed; at the appropriate time, have the students place their card at the correct location on the map or globe. Ask several students to come to the globe, find the approximate location of their state, and show the route from that state to the North Pole. Give students a map that shows North America and the North Pole. Have each student draw a line from various points in North America to the North Pole.

"Travel Poster"

After reading *How the Reindeer Saved Santa, How Santa Claus Had a Long and Difficult Journey Delivering His Presents, The Journey Home, Steam Train Ride,* and *King Island Christmas,* divide the class into groups of three or four. Provide each group with crayons, markers, large sheets of paper and tagboard, glue, old travel posters and brochures, magazines, and other art supplies. Tell students to plan an advertisement for a travel agency featuring a Christmas trip to the North Pole by train, car or bus, airplane, dogsled, or helicopter. Have the groups cooperatively plan the artwork and words for the travel poster. After the posters have been completed, display them around the room. Each group can then write a dialogue among a travel agent and prospective travelers. Set up a scene representing an office and have each group present its skit. This activity can be extended using the science activity "A Trip to the North Pole."

Activities for Creative Arts

"Bell Sounds"

Bring several sizes and types of bells to class. Ask various students to ring them one at a time. After describing the differences in the sounds made by the bells, remind the students of the importance of the sound of the bell in *The Polar Express*. Have the students describe Christmas events related to bells and other sounds that remind them of Christmas. Divide the students into groups of five. Give each group five baby-food jars, some teaspoons, and a pitcher of water. Instruct students to fill each of the five jars with a different amount of water, then tap each jar to hear the different tones. Using *The Fireside Book of Children's Songs,* sing several Christmas carols. Have the students try to produce the appropriate bell sound to accompany each song. Let each group prepare a song to be accompanied by the bells, and share the songs with the class.

"Polar Express Mural"

Attach a fifty four-by-twenty four-inch sheet of butcher paper to the classroom wall. Provide the class with art supplies for making elves, buildings, stars, reindeer, a train, Santa, and children. The completed mural will show what the North Pole looks like at midnight on Christmas Eve as Santa prepares to deliver gifts. Have one group of students draw the moon, stars, snow, sky, and buildings directly on the mural. Ask other students to draw elves, a train, Santa, reindeer, toys, and children on construction paper. Have them cut out the drawings and glue them to the mural. After the mural has been completed, the students should be encouraged to discuss how the mural relates to *The Polar Express*.

Have the students draw a picture showing how they spend or would like to spend Christmas Eve. Have them write sentences about the picture on the paper below the drawing.

Bulletin Boards

"The First Gift of Christmas"

Using the papers prepared in the language arts activity "First Gift of Christmas," have each student draw a picture of the gift. At the top of the bulletin board, place the heading *The First Gift of Christmas*. Cut four strips of Christmas wrapping paper. Mount them on the bulletin board to form an open box at the center of the board. Hang a real bell or a construction paper cutout in the center of the box. Have students mount their pictures on a piece of Christmas wrapping paper. Place these around the box on the bulletin board.

"We Celebrate on Christmas Eve"

Cover the bulletin board with green butcher paper cut in the shape of a Christmas tree. Make the tree larger than the bulletin board and fasten it to the wall. Cut the letters for the heading *We Celebrate on Christmas Eve* from Christmas wrapping paper. Mount the heading on the wall above the tree. Have the students glue their drawings and descriptions of Christmas Eve (from the creative arts activity "Polar Express Mural") on pieces of construction paper cut in the shape of a Christmas ornament. Place the ornaments on the bulletin board.

Related Books

Arnold, Caroline. *Maps and Globes: Fun, Facts, and Activities*. New York: Franklin Watts, 1984.
    This information book explains the use of maps and globes with instructions for projects, such as making a balloon globe, a model room, and a giant compass.

Berger, Melvin. *Seasons*. Illustrated by Ron Jones. New York: Doubleday, 1991.
    This book uses simple terms to explain the seasons and their effects on earth.

Carrick, Carol. *Paul's Christmas Birthday*. Illustrated by Donald Carrick. New York: Greenwillow Books, 1978.
    Paul's problem with a Christmas birthday is solved.

Compton, Kenn. *Happy Christmas to All*. New York: Holiday House, 1991.
    After a very tired Santa returns to the North Pole on Christmas Eve, he finds that Christmas morning holds a special surprise.

Gammell, Stephen. *Wake Up, Bear. . . It's Christmas!* New York: Lothrop, Lee & Shepard, 1981.
    This is a Christmas story about a bear who does not want to sleep.

Haywood, Carolyn. *How the Reindeer Saved Santa*. Illustrated by Victor G. Ambrus. New York: Morrow Junior Books, 1986.
    Santa has to be rescued by the reindeer after he trades his sleigh for a helicopter.

———. *Santa Claus Forever*. Illustrated by Glenys Ambrus and Victor Ambrus. New York: Morrow Junior Books, 1983.
    Santa decides not to retire when a suitable replacement cannot be found.

Hoban, Lillian. *It's Really Christmas*. New York: Greenwillow Books, 1982.
    A mouse angel teaches a lesson on the importance of other seasons in this story book.

Houston, Gloria. *The Year of the Perfect Christmas Tree*. Illustrated by Barbara Cooney. New York: Dial Books for Young Readers, 1988.
    After her father goes to war, a small girl and her mother provide the perfect Christmas tree for the village church. The story is set in Appalachia.

Impy, Rose. *A Letter to Santa Claus*. Illustrated by Susan Porter. New York: Bantam Books (Delacorte Press), 1988.
    Charlotte accidentally mails her mother's grocery list to Santa, and an interesting Christmas results.

Keller, Holly. *A Bear for Christmas*. New York: Greenwillow Books, 1986.
    A young boy cannot wait until Christmas to look at his Christmas gift.

Krahn, Fernando. *How Santa Claus Had a Long and Difficult Journey Delivering His Presents*. New York: Dell, 1988.
    Santa gets separated from his reindeer on Christmas Eve but is found in time to deliver the presents.

Leighton, M. *An Ellis Island Christmas*. Illustrated by Dennis Nolan. New York: Viking, 1992.
    The memories of a young immigrant's journey that ends on Christmas Eve at Ellis Island are revealed.

Lester, Alison. *The Journey Home*. New York: Houghton Mifflin, 1991.
    After digging a hole to the North Pole, two children journey through magical kingdoms home.

Lubin, Leonard. *Christmas Gift-Bringers*. New York: Lothrop, Lee & Shepard, 1989.
    Through an old book, a mouse learns the traditions of Christmas.

Lunn, Janet. *One Hundred Shining Candles*. Illustrated by Lindsay Grater. New York: Charles Scribner's Sons, 1991.
    Two children create a special Christmas gift.

Merriam, Eve. *The Christmas Box*. Illustrated by David Small. New York: Morrow Junior Books, 1985.
    A family of eleven finds a surprise under the Christmas tree on Christmas Day.

Mott, Evelyn C. *Steam Train Ride*. New York: Walker, 1991.
    Photographs tell the story of a ride on a steam train.

Patterson, Lillie. *Christmas in America*. Illustrated by Vincent Colabella. Champaign, Ill.: Garrard, 1969.
    This information book explains how the United States acquired some of its Christmas customs.

————. *Christmas in Britain and Scandinavia*. Illustrated by Kelly Oechsli. Champaign, Ill.: Garrard, 1970.
    This information book describes Christmas customs in the British Isles and Scandinavia.

Prelutsky, Jack. *It's Christmas*. Illustrated by Marylin Hafner. New York: Greenwillow Books, 1981.
    This collection of twelve Christmas poems reflects many Christmas interests.

Reiser, Lynn. *Christmas Counting*. New York: William Morrow (Greenwillow Books), 1992.
    A counting book for the Christmas season.

Rogers, Jean. *King Island Christmas*. Illustrated by Rie Munoz. New York: Greenwillow Books, 1985.
    This multicultural Christmas story tells how an Eskimo village rescues a priest who is stranded on a ship.

Spier, Peter. *Christmas*. New York: Bantam Books (Doubleday), 1983.
    This wordless picture book portrays all of the events and joys of the Christmas season through the delightful pictures.

Van Allsburg, Chris. *The Polar Express*. Illustrated by the author. Boston: Houghton Mifflin, 1985.
    On Christmas Eve, a young boy takes a magical train ride to the North Pole, where he receives the first gift of Christmas.

Van Rynbach, Iris. *Cecily's Christmas*. New York: Greenwillow Books, 1988.
    A humorous story about how Cecily shows the spirit of Christmas.

Winn, Marie. *The Fireside Book of Children's Songs*. New York: Simon & Schuster, 1966.
This collection has more than 100 songs, including nursery songs and games.

Yeomans, Thomas. *For Every Child a Star: A Christmas Story*. Illustrated by Tomie dePaola. New York: Holiday House, 1986.
This story tells of a discovery related to stars on Christmas Eve.

Zolotow, Charlotte. *The Beautiful Christmas Tree*. Illustrated by Ruth Robbins. Berkeley, Calif.: Parnassus, 1972.
This story divulges the loving transformation of an ugly tree into a beautiful Christmas tree.

Themes

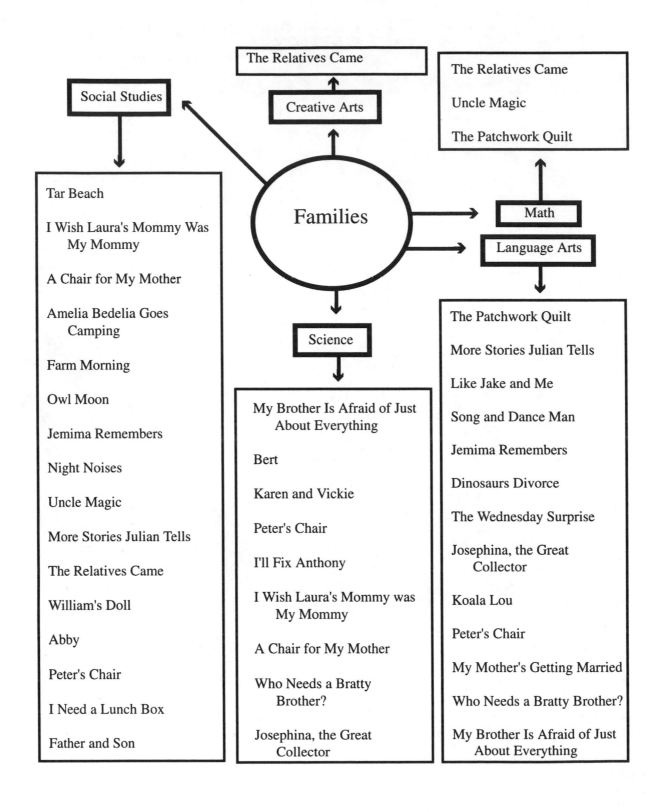

The Relatives Came

Social Studies

Creative Arts

Families

The Relatives Came

Uncle Magic

The Patchwork Quilt

Math

Language Arts

Science

Tar Beach

I Wish Laura's Mommy Was My Mommy

A Chair for My Mother

Amelia Bedelia Goes Camping

Farm Morning

Owl Moon

Jemima Remembers

Night Noises

Uncle Magic

More Stories Julian Tells

The Relatives Came

William's Doll

Abby

Peter's Chair

I Need a Lunch Box

Father and Son

My Brother Is Afraid of Just About Everything

Bert

Karen and Vickie

Peter's Chair

I'll Fix Anthony

I Wish Laura's Mommy was My Mommy

A Chair for My Mother

Who Needs a Bratty Brother?

Josephina, the Great Collector

The Patchwork Quilt

More Stories Julian Tells

Like Jake and Me

Song and Dance Man

Jemima Remembers

Dinosaurs Divorce

The Wednesday Surprise

Josephina, the Great Collector

Koala Lou

Peter's Chair

My Mother's Getting Married

Who Needs a Bratty Brother?

My Brother Is Afraid of Just About Everything

17

Families

ਨ

Genre: Realistic fiction

Summary: The books included in the bibliography show the special relationships in families, including adoption, divorce, and single-parent families, as well as intergenerational and sibling relationships.

Content Areas: Language arts, math, science, social studies, and creative arts. This theme can be used to introduce a social studies unit on families.

Brainstorming Starters:

Grandparent	Uncle
Mother	Divorce
Father	Weddings
Son	Adoption
Daughter	Only child
Cousin	Sibling rivalry
Aunt	Family life

Activities for Language Arts

"Family Newspaper"

As a beginning-of-the-year activity, read *The Patchwork Quilt*, *More Stories Julian Tells*, and *Like Jake and Me*. Allow students to describe various dwellings that serve as homes, such as apartments or mobile homes. Give each student a sheet of paper on which the outline of a house is drawn. Ask students to list the people who live in their home on the paper. Ask students to share their lists with the class. Have classmates listen to determine whether all of the families have the same number of individuals, children, or adults. Provide magazines, scissors, glue, and paper plates for students to create pictures of their families. Students can paste the pictures on the paper plates and share them with the class. Place the plates along the chalkboard for viewing. Have students identify the largest family, smallest family, the one with the most boys, and so forth. Have students write news items about their families in their journals for several days. At the end of the period, have students select one journal entry for publication in the class family newspaper. Have a selected group of students paste the items on sheets of paper to form a newspaper about class members' families. Place the newspaper in the reading center. This activity can be repeated throughout the year, rotating the group of "reporters" who assemble the newspaper.

"Relatives"

After reading *Song and Dance Man* and *Jemima Remembers*, have students identify the relatives mentioned in each story. Ask students to think about their relatives; list on the chalkboard the various relatives identified by class members, such as grandparents, aunts, uncles, cousins, stepbrothers, and stepsisters. As students explain each term, draw a diagram on the board to show the multiple relationships. Give pairs of students a card with a word or phrase such as *Mother's sister* or *Father's father*. Have the pair explain the relationship, and have one child in the pair introduce the other child to the class as the person identified on the card (i.e., "This is my mother's sister, my aunt.").

"Role-Play"

Read *Dinosaurs Divorce*; *The Wednesday Surprise*; *Josephina, the Great Collector*; *Koala Lou*; *Peter's Chair*; *My Mother's Getting Married*; *Who Needs a Bratty Brother?*, and *My Brother Is Afraid of Just About Everything*. Have students identify the problems revealed in each book. Divide students into groups to role-play a family situation. These might include the birth of a baby, the marriage of a parent, the selection of a new pet, or the death of a pet. After each role-play, discuss actions and possible alternatives.

Activities for Math

"Using Graphs"

Read *The Relatives Came* and *Uncle Magic* to identify relatives and relationships with relatives. Introduce the use of bar graphs by having students view various bar graphs that convey information related to the class, such as the number of boys and girls or the number of students in different classrooms (see page 155). Ask students to identify their favorite color, and list the totals for each color on the chalkboard. Show how these figures can be graphed by writing the names of the colors across the top of the chalkboard and placing a small square of colored paper representing each student's favorite color to form a column under the name of that color. Ask which color was selected by the most students, which was the least favorite color, and how many students liked a specific color.

After defining bar graphs and showing what kinds of information can be found on them, give each student a blank graph with the words *Brothers*, *Sisters*, *Aunts*, *Uncles*, *Cousins*, and *Grandparents* written across the bottom and with the numbers one through ten written in ascending order inside ten blocks stacked above each word (see page 156. Tell the students to complete the chart by coloring in the blocks above each word to represent the number of relatives they have in that category. For example, a student would fill in one block above *Brothers* if he or she has one brother and five blocks above *Aunts* if he or she has five aunts. Display the completed graphs, and have students use them to answer questions, for example, who has the most cousins or how many class members have no cousins.

(Text continues on page 157.)

FAVORITE COLORS

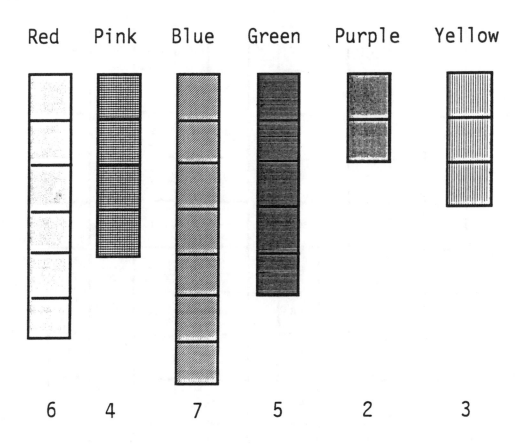

Red	Pink	Blue	Green	Purple	Yellow
6	4	7	5	2	3

RELATIVES

10	10	10	10	10	10
9	9	9	9	9	9
8	8	8	8	8	8
7	7	7	7	7	7
6	6	6	6	6	6
5	5	5	5	5	5
4	4	4	4	4	4
3	3	3	3	3	3
2	2	2	2	2	2
1	1	1	1	1	1
Brothers	Sisters	Aunts	Uncles	Cousins	Grandparents

"Equal Parts"

Read *The Patchwork Quilt.* Show pictures of different types of quilts, each picture labeled with the name of the quilt pattern. Call attention to the definite patterns of some quilts and also those with no particular pattern. Have students theorize how the patchwork quilt got its name. Divide the class into small groups; give each group the option of creating a quilt pattern or duplicating an existing one. Have each group create its pattern by cutting shapes from magazines or construction paper and gluing them on large sheets of butcher paper or construction paper.

Introduce the idea that dividing shapes into equal parts can be practiced using family groups. Show students pictures of families with three, four, five, and six members. Give each student four sheets of paper that are identical in size and shape. Encourage students to use crayons to draw a pie, cake, pizza, or some food product on the four sheets. Provide students with scissors. Direct them to cut apart one of the designs so that each member of the three-member family can have a piece. Have them compare the sizes of the three parts. Then ask them to try to cut the sheet for the four-member family into four equal pieces. Have the students place the pieces on top of each other to determine if the pieces are equal in size. Divide the class into small groups to cut the two remaining sheets of paper for the families of five and six members. Have individuals compare their pieces with those of other group members. When group comparisons have been made, give each student four sheets of paper on which a pie design has been divided into ten equal parts. For the first sheet, direct the students to color in the same number of "slices of pie" as there are students in the group. Then have them color one-half, one-tenth, and two-tenths of the pies on the remaining sheets. After comparing results, have students discuss times when families divide objects into equal parts.

Activities for Science

"Family Pets"

My Brother Is Afraid of Just About Everything and *Bert* can be used to introduce a study of family pets. Ask students to bring pictures of family pets to class or have them draw pictures of family pets. Have students volunteer to tell how the family got the pet, who is responsible for feeding or walking the pet, and what should be considered before getting a new pet. Following this discussion, divide the class into groups. Have each group devise a list of what a person should know before getting a pet. Also have each group decide on the perfect class pet. Have each group share its decision with the class and give reasons for the choice.

"Sharing Environmental Space Responsibly"

Karen and Vickie; *Peter's Chair*; *I'll Fix Anthony*; *Bert*; *I Wish Laura's Mommy Was My Mommy*; *A Chair for My Mother*; *Who Needs a Bratty Brother?*; and *Josephina, the Great Collector* can be used to help students understand the concepts of private space and sharing environmental space with other family members. Provide pictures of a child playing alone in a bedroom or playroom, a child dining with a larger family group, and a family completing household chores. Ask students to describe what is happening in each picture. Introduce the terms *responsibility*, *environmental space*, and *sharing space*. Ask how the future depends on how we care for the environment. Ask students to think about the classroom environment and brainstorm ways to care for it. After making a list of ways to care for the classroom, make a chart of responsibilities with each student selecting a task and being assigned a day to complete it. Discuss different spaces in the home, such as kitchen, bedrooms, and living room, and have students discuss who takes care of these spaces. After the students have selected a helping task to do at home, give students blank coupons on which to write "I will help preserve my home environment by (name of task, i.e., washing dishes). Have students complete the coupons and present them to parents or caretakers.

Activities for Social Studies

"Family Careers"

Read *Tar Beach, I Wish Laura's Mommy Was My Mommy*, and *A Chair for My Mother* and discuss the term *career*. Have students discuss tasks family members perform at home and on the job. Have students collect two sets of pictures from magazines: one set of adults at work and one set of adults performing tasks at home. Have students share the pictures and discuss the jobs identified in them. Make a chart listing the different jobs that were identified, and discuss the importance of each job.

"Things Families Do Together"

After sharing *Amelia Bedelia Goes Camping, Farm Morning, Father and Son, Owl Moon, Jemima Remembers, Night Noises*, and *Uncle Magic*, have the class brainstorm activities that families can do together. List these activities under the headings *Working Together* and *Having Fun*. Ask students to think silently for a few minutes about a conversation that they had with a family member while working or playing together and a conversation that they would like to have with a family member. Ask the students to write about either thought. Have volunteers share their work with the class.

"Traveling with Family Members"

Jemima Remembers, More Stories Julian Tells, Amelia Bedelia Goes Camping, and *The Relatives Came* can be used as a springboard for planning vacation trips. Hang a large map of the United States on the bulletin board. After discussions with classmates and relatives, and looking at the map, ask students to choose places in the United States that they would like to go with their family on vacation. Have students write their name and the name of a city on a piece of paper cut in the shape of a car or airplane, then pin the car or airplane on that location on a large map of the United States. Distribute smaller maps of the country, and have each student identify all of the locations that were identified on the large map. Encourage students to find pictures, brochures, and other information about their chosen location to share with class members. In small groups, have students research and discuss information about one of the locations. Have each group decide on a perfect souvenir from that location and draw or find a picture of it. Give each group the opportunity to share its picture with the class.

"Me Book"

William's Doll, Abby, Peter's Chair, and *I Need a Lunch Box* can be used to encourage students to think about themselves. Have students complete a questionnaire with words or drawings. Include questions such as "My favorite food is. . ."; "I like to play...."; "My telephone number is. . ."; "My favorite toy is. . ."; and "I have. . .brothers and. . .sisters." Provide blank sheets of paper cut in the shape of a boy or girl. Encourage students to use the questionnaire as they draw pictures and write (or, for younger children, dictate) sentences on the blank sheets of the book. Fasten all sheets together and write *Book About Me* by. . . on the title page. Ask volunteers to read their books and to share them with classmates. Display the books in the reading center before allowing students to take the books home.

Activities for Creative Arts

"Family Portrait"

After reading *The Relatives Came*, provide craft sticks, paper, crayons, and fabrics for making stick-puppet family portraits. Have students decorate stick figures to represent each member of their family. A styrofoam board can be used to position the puppets. Have students make a name tag for each puppet and write a brief paragraph to go with each one. Display the puppets and the paragraphs in the classroom.

Bulletin Boards

"Family Vacations"
Place a large map of the United States on the bulletin board. Above the map place the heading *Family Vacations*. As described in the social studies activity "Traveling with Family Members," each student will place his or her car or airplane figure at the correct location on the map. The souvenir pictures selected by the groups in the same activity can be placed around the map.

"Family Careers"
In the center of the bulletin board, place the heading *Family Careers*. On either side, place the headings *On the Job* and *Jobs at Home*. Have students place the pictures collected in the social studies activity "Family Careers" under the proper headings. Have students write their names beside a job they would like to do when they grow up.

Related Books

Ackerman, Karen. *Song and Dance Man*. Illustrated by Stephen Gammell. New York: Alfred A. Knopf, 1988. (Caldecott Medal)
    Grandpa demonstrates songs and dances and tells jokes from his vaudeville act.

Brown, Laurene Krasny and Marc Brown. *Dinosaurs Divorce*. Illustrated by the authors. Boston: Little, Brown (Joy Street Books), 1986.
    With humorous dinosaur drawings this book gives straightforward truths about divorce and its effect on the child.

Bunting, Eve. *The Wednesday Surprise*. Illustrated by Donald Carrick. Boston: Houghton Mifflin (Clarion Books), 1989.
    Dad receives a surprise for his birthday when seven-year-old Anna teaches grandma to read.

Caines, Jeannette. *Abby*. Illustrated by Steven Kellogg. New York: Harper & Row, 1973.
    A black girl learns she is adopted.

———. *I Need a Lunch Box*. Illustrated by Pat Cummings. New York: Harper & Row, 1988.
A young black boy wants a lunch box like his older sister.

Cameron, Ann. *More Stories Julian Tells*. Illustrated by Ann Strugnell. New York: Alfred A. Knopf, 1986.
This book contains seven stories about the everyday adventures of a black family and friends.

Dragonwagon, Crescent. *Jemima Remembers*. Illustrated by Troy Howell. New York: Macmillan, 1984.
Jemima remembers a special summer spent with her aunt.

Drescher, Joan. *My Mother's Getting Married*. Illustrated by the author. New York: Dial Books for Young Readers, 1986.
Katie's worries about her mother's marriage to Ben are resolved after her whole class comes to the wedding.

Engel, Diana. *Josephina, the Great Collector*. Illustrated by the author. New York: William Morrow, 1988.
Josephina is a collector, and her sister is not. Josephina comes up with a creative solution to their problems.

Flourney, Valerie. *The Patchwork Quilt*. Illustrated by Jerry Pinkney. New York: Dial Books for Young Readers, 1986.
A loving black family's daily life is told through a patchwork quilt of memories.

Fox, Mem. *Koala Lou*. Illustrated by Pamela Lofts. New York: Harcourt Brace Jovanovich (Gulliver Books), 1988.
This is the story of sibling rivalry and how the oldest Koala plans to win her mother's attention and affection by entering a sporting event..

———. *Night Noises*. Illustrated by Terry Denton. New York: Harcourt Brace Jovanovich (Voyager Books), 1989.
Lily Laceby is almost ninety. She dozes off and is pleasantly surprised by her family when she awakens.

Gauch, Patricia Lee. *Uncle Magic*. Illustrated by Deborah Kogan Ray. New York: Holiday House, 1992.
A little girl's uncle creates a time of magic.

Gondosch, Linda. *Who Needs a Bratty Brother?* Illustrated by Helen Cogancherry. New York: E. P. Dutton (Lodestar Books), 1985.
Kelly has a brother who does things to drive her wild.

Jukes, Mavis. *Like Jake and Me*. Illustrated by Lloyd Bloom. New York: Alfred A. Knopf (Borzoi Books), 1984. (Newbery Honor)
A stepfamily finds the things that happen to them bind them together.

Keats, Ezra Jack. *Peter's Chair*. New York: Harper & Row, 1967.
Peter feels that his new baby sister has usurped his rights and possessions.

Lauture, Denize. *Father and Son*. Illustrated by Jonathan Green. New York: Putnam (Philomel), 1992.
A father and son share special times.

McHugh, Elisabet. *Karen and Vickie*. New York: Greenwillow Books, 1984.
Stepsisters must share a room after a baby is born.

McPhail, David. *Farm Morning*. San Diego, Calif.: Harcourt Brace Jovanovich, 1985.
The bonds of affection between a girl and her father are conveyed as she ineptly helps with the chores.

Osborn, Lois. *My Brother Is Afraid of Just About Everything*. Illustrated by Jennie Williams. Niles, Ill.: Albert Whitman, 1982.
An older brother cannot understand his younger brother's fears until a huge dog happens by.

Parish, Peggy. *Amelia Bedelia Goes Camping*. New York: Greenwillow Books, 1985.
Amelia Bedelia and her family go on a camping trip that has many laughs as Amelia Bedelia carefully and literally follows instructions.

Power, Barbara. *I Wish Laura's Mommy Was My Mommy*. Illustrated by Marylin Hafner. New York: J. B. Lippincott, 1979.
When a young girl trades mothers for a short time, she gets a better understanding of her own mother.

Ringgold, Faith. *Tar Beach*. Illustrated by the author. New York: Crown, 1991.
A young girl dreams about owning all of the buildings in her city, especially her father's job site.

Rylant, Cynthia. *The Relatives Came*. Illustrated by Stephen Gammell. New York: Bradbury Press, 1985. (Caldecott Honor)
The relatives from Virginia come to visit in a station wagon, and everyone had a wonderful time as one huge, happy family.

Skulavik, Mary A. *Bert*. Illustrated by Zofia Kostyrko. New York: Walker, 1990.
Timmy plots to get rid of the new family computer because it is getting more praise and attention.

Viorst, Judith. *I'll Fix Anthony*. Illustrated by Arnold Lobel. New York: Harper & Row, 1969.
A boy brags about how he is going to fix his older, arrogant big brother, Anthony, who makes life miserable.

Williams, Vera B. *A Chair for My Mother*. New York: Mulberry Books, 1982. (Caldecott Honor)
After a fire destroys their furniture, a child, her mother, and her grandmother save dimes to buy a chair.

Yolen, Jane. *Owl Moon*. Illustrated by John Schoenherr. New York: Philomel, 1987.
A girl and her father take a cold, quiet walk on a moonlit night, looking for an owl.

Zolotow, Charlotte. *William's Doll*. Illustrated by William Pene du Bois. New York: Harper & Row, 1974.
A grandmother understands that little boys as well as little girls can learn to care from playing with a doll.

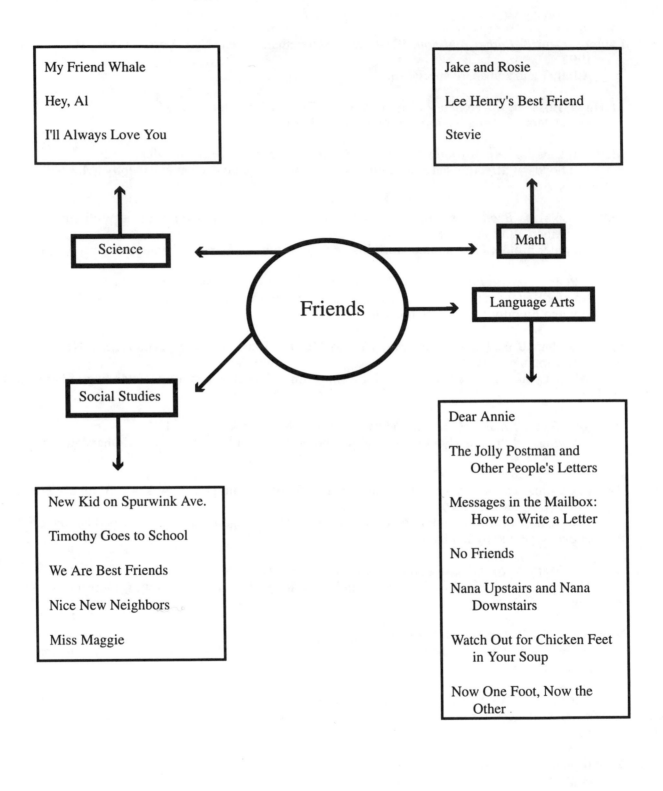

My Friend Whale

Hey, Al

I'll Always Love You

Jake and Rosie

Lee Henry's Best Friend

Stevie

Science

Math

Friends

Language Arts

Social Studies

New Kid on Spurwink Ave.

Timothy Goes to School

We Are Best Friends

Nice New Neighbors

Miss Maggie

Dear Annie

The Jolly Postman and
    Other People's Letters

Messages in the Mailbox:
    How to Write a Letter

No Friends

Nana Upstairs and Nana
    Downstairs

Watch Out for Chicken Feet
    in Your Soup

Now One Foot, Now the
    Other

18

Friends

ঽ

Genre: Picture books

Summary: The books included in the bibliography show the special relationships of many kinds of friends, including animals, family members, best friends, school friends, and friends with disabilities.

Content Areas: Language arts, math, science, social studies, and creative arts. These books will be useful in a social studies unit about friendship.

Brainstorming Starters:

Grandparents	Friends
Cousins	Best friends
Dogs	Friends with special problems
Cats	School friends
Neighbors	Making friends

Activities for Language Arts

"Friendly Letters or Pen Pal Letters"

Read aloud *Dear Annie*, *The Jolly Postman and Other People's Letters*, and *Messages in the Mailbox: How to Write a Letter*. Prepare a chart to show the format of a friendly letter (see page 164). Have students write to a classmate who has recently moved or has been absent. Before writing the letters, have students draw pictures of themselves showing how they felt when the friend moved away or was absent. This will help students focus on the memory of the friend. During the class period, students also could practice writing letters to each other; they could proof and revise these letters. The letter to be mailed to the former or sick classmate is the final product. A related activity might involve writing to pen pals from another school in a distant city.

"Simulated Journal"

Based on *No Friends* or another book on friendship, have the students role-play a character (i.e., Grandpa in *No Friends*) as they write a brief, simulated journal, writing the entries from the viewpoint of the character. If the character is not a child in the book, the viewpoint of that character should be when he or she was a child.

Scott Traverse
15 Dixie
Duncan, MS 39402
May 30, 1994

←▪ ▪ ▪ ▪ Return address

Dear John,

←▪ ▪ ▪ ▪ ▪ ▪ ▪ ▪ Greeting

We miss you. Do you
like your new school?

←▪ ▪ ▪ ▪ ▪ ▪ ▪ ▪ Body

Your pal,
Scott

←▪ ▪ ▪ ▪ ▪ ▪ ▪ ▪ Closing

"Grandparents"

Write the word *grandparent* on the chalkboard and ask students to think of other names people call their grandparents. Have students read aloud *Nana Upstairs and Nana Downstairs*, *Watch Out for Chicken Feet in Your Soup*, and *Now One Foot, Now the Other*. Discuss the characters in the books. Have student write individual stories about something special they have done with a grandparent. In small groups, have the students retell the stories in their own words.

Activities for Math

"A Visit with Friends"

Read *Jake and Rosie*, *Lee Henry's Best Friend*, and *Stevie*. Have students describe the friendship portrayed in each story. Use poster board or tagboard to develop a game entitled "A Visit with Friends" for the math center (see page 165). Draw three rows of four squares each to represent houses. Name the streets, and assign children's names and house numbers to each block. In the lower left block print *Start*, and in the upper right block print *Home*. Use small toys as playing pieces. Print arithmetic problems on three-by-five-inch cards. On each card print the numerals l, 2, or 3, indicating the number of squares to be moved if the player gives the correct answer. Have each player take turns drawing a card and solving the arithmetic problem. The object of the game is to reach Home.

A VISIT WITH FRIENDS

Question Cards			

4th Avenue

Home 109	Sue's 216	Bob's 307

3rd Avenue

Bill's 107	Street	Tim's 214	Street	Pat's 305	Street

2nd Avenue

Ann's 105	School	Joy's 212	Friendly	Kim's 303	Main

1st Avenue

Mike's 103	Joe's 210	School 301

START

Activities for Science

"Pets"

After reading and discussing the themes of *My Friend Whale*; *Hey, Al*; and *I'll Always Love You,* place pictures of animals on the science table. Include pictures of endangered species, wild animals, and household pets. Working at the science table, students can select one of the pictures and research information about the animal. Have students classify the animal as endangered, wild, or pet and share information learned about the animal with the class.

In a related activity, have each student pick one animal and tell why that animal would make a good friend. Have each student name the animal and draw a picture and write a story about an experience with the animal. Place the pictures and stories in the science center.

Activities for Social Studies

"Friendly Words"

After reading *New Kid on Spurwink Ave.*, *Timothy Goes to School*, or *We Are Best Friends*, divide students into cooperative groups to brainstorm words that convey friendship and words that help friendships grow, for example, "Do you want to play?" or "I'm sorry." Have each group present its list to the class. Students can then role-play situations in which they or their friends have used friendly words to improve a friendship.

"Friendly Pictures"

Discuss several books on friendship. Have students form cooperative groups. Give each group several pictures showing situations involving various people. Have the groups select the pictures that show friendships and friendly actions. Have groups share the selected pictures by explaining the actions related to friendship in each one.

"Rules of Friendship"

Following the "Friendly Words" and "Friendly Pictures" activities, have students create a bulletin board relating the rules of friendship. Have the class brainstorm to develop rules for friendships; list the rules on chart paper. Place the chart on the bulletin board. Have the students draw a picture or write a sentence about "how to be a friend." Place the pictures and sentences on the bulletin board under the phrase *Rules for Friendship*.

"Neighborhood Map"

After discussing the books *Nice New Neighbors* and *Miss Maggie*, have students retell the stories. Have students cut out two houses from construction paper—one for themselves and one for their best friend in the neighborhood. Have the class make one large map of the neighborhood on butcher paper, including street names see page 167). Have students paste their house and their friend's house on the map. If the best friends are classmates, avoid duplication of houses on the map by having students place their own house on the map and giving their second house to the appropriate classmate.

NEIGHBORHOOD MAP

Mary		School

Pennsylvania Avenue

John	Heather Mary's Friend	

Chesterfield Road

Jay Road

Meghan	Jacob	Stacy Robert's Friend

University Drive

South 34th Street

Southern Lane

Robert	Bill John's Friend	

Activities for Creative Arts

"Frieze"

Have students cut out the pictures of the animals they drew as part of the science activity "Pets." Paste the pictures on long, narrow strips of butcher paper to form a frieze. Display the frieze in the science center.

"Role-Play"

Arrange students into the cooperative groups formed for the social studies activity "Friendly Pictures." Have the groups select one of the friendly pictures and role-play the situation for the class. Have the class discuss each scenario. Tape the dramatizations on audiotape or videotape. This activity encourages socialization skills development.

Bulletin Boards

"Pet"
Across the top of the bulletin board, write the phrase *Our Pets*. Place strips of construction paper vertically on the bulletin board. Each strip represents a category of pet, such as dog, cat, or fish. Place pictures of students' pets on the appropriate strip. In the center of the board, hang a graph that shows the number and type of students' pets.

"Family"
Gather the stories students wrote as part of the language arts activity "Grandparents." Have students bring in pictures of their grandparents to go with the stories. Display the pictures with the stories under the heading *Our Grandparents*.

Related Books

Animal Friends

James, Simon. *My Friend Whale*. New York: Bantam Books, 1991.
  Awareness of an endangered species is developed through the friendship of a boy and a blue whale.

Wilhelm, Hans. *I'll Always Love You*. Illustrated by the author. New York: Crown, 1985.
  A young boy's grief over the death of his dog is eased by the fact that he had told her every night, "I'll always love you."

Yorinks, Arthur. *Hey, Al*. Illustrated by Richard Egielski. New York: Farrar, Straus & Giroux, 1986.
  Al, a janitor, and his faithful dog, Eddie, leave their mundane lives behind for a taste of paradise.

Supplemental Reading

Lobel, Arnold. *Frog and Toad Are Friends*. Illustrated by the author. New York: Harper & Row, 1970.
  The story continues the devoted friendship of Frog and Toad.

McLerran, Alice. *I Want to Go Home*. Illustrated by J. Kastner. New York: William Morrow (Tambourine Books), 1992.
  Marta has difficulty adjusting to her new home, but Sammy, a cat, diverts her attention.

Rylant, Cynthia. *Henry and Mudge: The First Book of Their Adventure*. Illustrated by Sucil Stevenson. New York: Bradbury Press, 1987.
  The story of Henry's adventures with his dog, Mudge.

Sharmat, Marjorie Wienman. *The 329th Friend*. Illustrated by Cyndy Szekeres. New York: Four Winds Press, 1992.
  Emery Raccoon invites 328 guests to his party but enjoys his own company best.

Wilhelm, Hans. *A New Home, a New Friend*. New York: Random House, 1985.
  A boy adapts to a new home with the help of an abandoned dog.

Williams, Margery. *The Velveteen Rabbit*. Illustrated by W. Nicholson. New York: Doubleday, n.d.
  A child's love for a stuffed rabbit results in magic.

Best Friends

Aliki. *We Are Best Friends*. New York: Greenwillow Books, 1982.
  Two friends separated by a move find new friends but also remain friends.

Delton, Judy. *Lee Henry's Best Friend*. Illustrated by John Faulkner. Chicago: Albert Whitman, 1980.
  Lee Henry finds he can make another friend when his best friend moves away.

Lillie, Patricia. *Jake and Rosie*. New York: Greenwillow Books, 1989.
  Jake's best friend, Rosie, has a nice surprise for him.

Merriam, Eve. *Fighting Words*. Illustrated by David Small. New York: Morrow Junior Books, 1992.
  Two best friends argue.

Steptoe, John. *Stevie*. New York: Harper & Row, 1969.
This is the story of a friendship between two boys.

Supplemental Reading

Merriam, Eve. *Fighting Words*. Illustrated by David Small. New York: Morrow Junior Books, 1992.
Two best friends argue.

Udry, J. M. *Let's Be Enemies*. Pictures by Maurice Sendak. New York: Scholastic, 1961.
Two boys fight over possessions, but when the sun comes out, they go off arm in arm.

Waber, Bernard. *Ira Sleeps Over*. Illustrated by the author. Boston: Houghton Mifflin, 1988.
Ira feels terrible when he learns that his friend Reggie is going to move away.

Winthrop, Elizabeth. *Katherine's Doll*. Illustrated by Marylin Hafner. New York: E. P. Dutton, 1983.
Two girls who become jealous over a doll learn that a doll cannot take the place of a best friend.

Family Friends

Caseley, Judith. *Dear Annie*. New York: Greenwillow Books, 1991.
Annie and her grandfather exchange postcards and letters from the date of her birth.

dePaola, Tomie. *Nana Upstairs and Nana Downstairs*. New York: Putnam, 1973.
This is the story of a boy's relationship with his grandmother and great-grandmother.

————. *Now One Foot, Now the Other*. New York: Putnam, 1981.
Roles are reversed as a grandson helps his grandfather recover from a stroke.

————. *Watch Out for Chicken Feet in Your Soup*. Englewood Cliffs, N.J.: Prentice-Hall, 1974.
An old-fashioned Italian grandmother shows affection for her grandson.

Supplemental Reading

Hines, Anna Grossnickle. *Jackie's Lunch Box*. New York: Greenwillow Books, 1991.
Jackie prepares a surprise for her older sister who is away at school.

Keats, Ezra Jack. *Peter's Chair*. New York: Harper & Row, 1967.
Peter feels his rights and possessions are usurped by a baby sister.

McCloskey, Robert. *Blueberries for Sal*. New York: Viking, 1948.
Sal and her mother, berry-picking on a hillside, meet a mother bear and her cub who eat the berries.

Viorst, Judith. *I'll Fix Anthony*. Illustrated by Arnold Lobel.
New York: Harper & Row, 1969.
A boy brags about how he is going to fix his arrogant big brother, who makes life miserable.

Yolen, Jane. *Owl Moon*. New York: Philomel, 1987. (Caldecott Award)
A girl and her father take a cold, quiet walk on a moonlit night, looking for an owl.

Neighborhood Friends

Brandenberg, F. *Nice New Neighbors*. Illustrated by Aliki. New York: Greenwillow Books, 1977.
A family of field mice makes friends in a new neighborhood.

Crowley, Michael. *New Kid on Spurwink Ave.* Illustrated by Abby Carter. Boston: Little, Brown, 1992.
  A new kid seems boring until the other kids discover his special interest.

Rylant, Cynthia. *Miss Maggie.* Illustrated by Thomas Di Grazia. New York: E. P. Dutton, 1983.
  Miss Maggie, an aging recluse, lives across the field from Nat and his grandmother.

Stevenson, James. *No Friends.* New York: Greenwillow Books, 1986.
  Grandpa helps Mary Ann and Louise adjust to their new neighborhood with stories of his move as a child.

School Friends

Ahlberg, Janet, and Allan Ahlberg. *The Jolly Postman and Other People's Letters.* Illustrated by the authors. Boston: Little, Brown, 1986.
  The jolly postman delivers letters to fairy-tale characters; the letters come in envelopes that can be easily opened.

Leedy, Loreen. *Messages in the Mailbox: How to Write a Letter.* Illustrated by the author. New York: Holiday House, 1991.
  A teacher introduces her class to the art of letter-writing in all its forms, from fun to business.

Wells, Rosemary. *Timothy Goes to School.* New York: Dial Books for Young Readers, 1985.
  Timothy finds acceptance and makes friends.

Supplemental Reading

Allard, Harry. *Miss Nelson Is Missing.* Illustrated by James Marshall. Boston: Houghton Mifflin, 1977.
  The students in room 207 learn to appreciate their teacher after Viola Swamp serves as a substitute for Miss Nelson.

Blume, Judy. *Freckle Juice.* Illustrated by Sonia O. Lisker. New York: Four Winds Press, 1971.
  A gullible second-grader pays fifty cents for a recipe to grow freckles.

Henkes, Kevin. *Jessica.* New York: Greenwillow Books, 1989.
  At kindergarten, Jessica meets a friend with the same name as her imaginary friend.

Special Friends

Supplemental Reading

Clifton, Lucille. *My Friend Jacob.* Illustrated by Thomas Di Grazia. New York: E. P. Dutton, 1980.
  This is a story about a friendship with a disabled person.

Rosenberg, Maxine B. *My Friend Leslie: The Story of a Handicapped Child.* Photography by George Ancona. New York: Lothrop, Lee & Shepard, 1983.
  This is a true story about a disabled child.

Russo, Marisabina. *Alex Is My Friend. New York: William Morrow (Greenwillow Books), 1992.*
  A handicap does not limit the friendship of Alex and Ben.

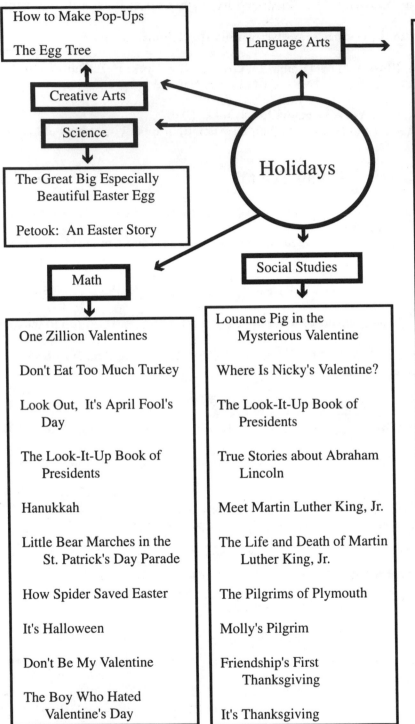

How to Make Pop-Ups

The Egg Tree

Creative Arts

Science

The Great Big Especially
Beautiful Easter Egg

Petook: An Easter Story

Math

One Zillion Valentines

Don't Eat Too Much Turkey

Look Out, It's April Fool's
Day

The Look-It-Up Book of
Presidents

Hanukkah

Little Bear Marches in the
St. Patrick's Day Parade

How Spider Saved Easter

It's Halloween

Don't Be My Valentine

The Boy Who Hated
Valentine's Day

Language Arts

Holidays

Social Studies

Louanne Pig in the
Mysterious Valentine

Where Is Nicky's Valentine?

The Look-It-Up Book of
Presidents

True Stories about Abraham
Lincoln

Meet Martin Luther King, Jr.

The Life and Death of Martin
Luther King, Jr.

The Pilgrims of Plymouth

Molly's Pilgrim

Friendship's First
Thanksgiving

It's Thanksgiving

Hubknuckles

How Spider Saved Easter

The Egg Tree

Ghost's Hour, Spook's Hour

I Love Passover

There's No Such Thing as a
Chanukah Bush, Sandy
Goldstein

Jeremy Bean's St. Patrick's
Day

Little Bear Marches in the
St. Patrick's Day Parade

Fried Feathers for
Thanksgiving

Don't Eat Too Much Turkey

Bee My Valentine

The Little Old Lady Who
Was Not Afraid of
Anything

Funnybones

The Ghost Train

Spooky and the Ghost Cat

19

Holidays

ॐ

Genre: Picture book

Summary: The books included in the bibliography show how holidays are celebrated. Holidays highlighted include Presidents' Day, Valentines Day, Martin Luther King Day, Arbor Day, Earth Day, April Fool's Day, and traditional Christian and Jewish holidays.

Content Areas: Language arts, math, science, social studies, and creative arts. These books can be used to introduce a unit on a specific holiday or on holidays and traditions in general.

Brainstorming Starters:

Celebrate	Arbor Day
Memories	Presidents' Day
Traditions	Martin Luther King Day
Family traditions	Thanksgiving
Keeping traditions	Halloween
Holidays	Hanukkah
Holiday foods	Passover
Gifts	Easter
Chanukah Bush	Father's Day
Valentines Day	Mother's Day
April Fools Day	St. Patrick's Day
May Day'	

Activities for Language Arts

"Making a Big Book"

After reading books related to a particular holiday (or several holidays), such as *How Spider Saved Easter*, or *Hubknuckles*, introduce the idea of making a big book as a way to share an original group story about a holiday event. Describe a big book and how to construct one before having volunteers suggest titles or subjects for a big book. Write the suggestions for titles or topics on the chalkboard. Have students choose one or two of the titles or topics and divide the class into groups based on students' first or second choice. Provide art supplies, such as large sheets of chart paper, crayons, tempera paints, pictures, and pens. Give instructions for writing the story and for binding, making the cover and title page, inserting the text, and adding illustrations. Suggest that each student in the group contribute to the big book by participating in composing the story; then have the group divide the responsibility for completing the pages among group members. Assist students as they develop the story and write it out. When the books have been completed, have each group share its story with the class before placing the books in the reading center or sharing them with other classes. Students may also make big-book replicas of holiday picture books.

"Identifying School Holidays"

Brainstorm to find out which holidays that occur during the school year can be identified by the class. Make a chart that shows the holidays celebrated during the school year. Write the words *memories* and *traditions* on the chalkboard and ask students to think about their meanings. Have children share memories of family events, school, or vacations. Discuss traditions and have students suggest ways that activities become traditions. Following a discussion of the terms, have students write about a holiday memory or a tradition observed in their family. Ask volunteers to share ideas developed during the writing activity.

Display and introduce *The Egg Tree*; *Ghost's Hour, Spook's Hour*; *I Love Passover*; *There's No Such Thing as a Chanukah Bush, Sandy Goldstein*; and *Jeremy Bean's St. Patrick's Day*. Provide time for students to read at least one of the books, and then divide the class into groups to discuss the traditions or memories in the books. After identifying the holidays and the associated traditions, ask the groups to invent a holiday and a tradition for it. Provide art supplies and have each group construct a picture book about the invented holiday. Each group may exchange its picture book with other groups. Place the finished products in the reading center.

"Predicting from Titles"

Display some or all of the following books: *Little Bear Marches in the St. Patrick's Day Parade*, *Fried Feathers for Thanksgiving*, *Don't Eat Too Much Turkey*, *Friendship's First Thanksgiving*, *Bee My Valentine*, *The Little Old Lady Who Was Not Afraid of Anything*, *Funnybones*, *The Ghost Train*, and *Spooky and the Ghost Cat*. (You may wish to display only those titles related to one holiday.) Ask the students to look at the titles and think about what might happen in the story. Have the students choose one of the books and write a prediction of the plot. Have each student read the selected story, write a short summary of the plot, and evaluate his or her prediction. Discuss the stories and ask who predicted the plot or theme correctly. Divide the class into groups to write a new chapter or ending for one of the books. Have each group share its work with the class. Put the chapters together and place them in the reading center.

Activities for Math

"Sequence the Holidays"

Introduce a study of sequencing by displaying *One Zillion Valentines*; *Don't Eat Too Much Turkey*; *Look Out, It's April Fool's Day*; *The Look-It-Up Book of Presidents*; *Hanukkah*; *Little Bear Marches in the St. Patrick's Day Parade*; *How Spider Saved Easter*; and *It's Halloween* on a table. Hold up pictures of these holidays and have volunteers match each picture with the appropriate book. Ask students to fold a sheet of paper to make eight sections. Have them write one holiday in each section. Show the students a large year-long calendar and tell them the books represent holidays that occur during the school year. Group the students in pairs. Have each pair cut one of the sectioned papers apart and place the holidays in the order in which they occur during the school year. Write the date of each holiday on the large calendar and discuss the dates with the class. Have the pairs verify the sequence in which they ordered the slips of paper on which the names of the holidays were written. Provide calendars of each month of the school year, scissors, and glue. Have the students glue the slips of paper onto the correct date. Other information can be added to the calendars to remind students of the sequence of school holidays. Allow the students to take the calendars home.

"How Many Valentines?"

Read *One Zillion Valentines*. Write the word *zillion* on the board. Ask how many a zillion is and accept the students' answers before revealing it is a very large number. Have students describe situations in which knowing an exact number is important. Ask how many valentines would be needed for a Valentine's Day party if everyone in the classroom received two cards from each person. Record various estimates on the board and plan to check them after the group activity described later in this paragraph. Read *Don't Be My Valentine* and *The Boy Who Hated Valentine's Day*. Ask students how many valentines they expect to receive and what it would feel like if no one gave them a valentine. Discuss sharing valentines. Divide the class into groups to determine the total number of valentines needed if each student in the class is to receive two valentines. Determine the correct answer (take into account that students will send valentines to each other but not to themselves) and compare it to the earlier estimates. Provide art supplies for making valentines bearing messages and addition and subtraction problems that have answers one through twenty. Write the phrase *How Many Valentines?* on a bulletin board and have students place their valentines on the board. Have students select several valentines from the bulletin board and solve the arithmetic problems by drawing the number of valentines that correctly answers the problems. Students may work in pairs to check their work.

Activities for Science

"Spring Fever"

Write the terms *Earth Day* and *Arbor Day* on the board. Show pictures related to each. Ask students to identify the time of the year the holidays occur and tell what the names of the holidays mean. After students discuss the relationship of the holidays to spring, trees, and caring for the earth, have them find information about how the celebrations began and how we celebrate the holidays today. Have groups of students draw pictures or plan activities to protect trees and the planet. The pictures and activities can be displayed on a large chart. Have each student select one of the activities to do. Distribute a calendar for the current month and have students write a reminder to do the activity. Schedule a day to clean up the classroom or playground to emphasize the importance of being responsible for completing the selected activities.

"Eggs"

Read *The Great Big Especially Beautiful Easter Egg* and *Petook: An Easter Story*. Have students describe the different roles of the egg in each book. Introduce a study of eggs by displaying several kinds of eggs along with paired pictures of eggs and baby animals. Ask students to look at the pictures and identify the differences among the eggs. After pointing out differences, have the students match an egg with the baby animal hatched from that egg. Encourage students to use resource books and encyclopedias to verify their guesses. Brainstorm to find what students know about eggs. Introduce eggs as symbols of birth and the beginning of a life cycle. Divide the class into groups; give each group a hard-boiled egg and a raw egg. Have the students observe the eggs' oval shape before peeling the hard-boiled egg and cutting it in half. Help them break the raw egg into a cup. Show a large diagram of an egg with the parts labeled. Have the students identify the parts by observing the hard-boiled and raw eggs. Ask each group to draw an egg and label the shell, membrane, white, and yolk. Have students identify and discuss the function of each part, tell how an embryo develops, and find information about eggs, including the number of eggs laid by various animals and the incubation period for them. Use charts labeled with pictures of specific eggs to share facts about those eggs.

Activities for Social Studies

"The Mail System"

Use Valentine's Day to introduce a study of the mail system. Read *Louanne Pig in the Mysterious Valentine* and *Where Is Nicky's Valentine?* and discuss the giving and receiving of valentines. As the class prepares to distribute valentines, have each student make a small mailbox from a shoe box or other small box. After writing their addresses on the mailboxes, have students brainstorm reasons for using an address. Expand beyond ideas related to obtaining correspondence by the postal service, for example, catalog shopping, pizza deliveries, or private delivery services, such as United Parcel Service. Ask a mail carrier, clerk, or other resource person to explain to the class how the mail system works. In preparation for the resource person's visit, divide the class into groups to research the mail system; to find pictures of mailboxes, postal workers, or postal vehicles; and to bring stamps or stamp collections to class. Have groups share their findings with the class and develop questions for the resource person. Have the students share information they learned from the resource person by drawing pictures or writing fact sheets about the mail system.

"Presidents' Day"

Display *The Look-It Up Book of Presidents*, *True Stories About Abraham Lincoln*, a penny, a one-dollar bill, pictures of the Washington and Lincoln memorials, and other materials related to George Washington and Abraham Lincoln. Ask the students what these items have in common. On a calendar, point out the men's birthdays and introduce Presidents' Day as a day for honoring the two presidents. Provide each student with a blank calendar for the month of February. Have each student mark Washington's and Lincoln's birthdays and also mark the third Monday in February as Presidents' Day.

Ask students to work in pairs to research facts and legends about each man. Record the students' findings on a chart. Divide the class into groups to determine the accuracy of the information on the chart, find additional facts about each man, list the accomplishments of each, and determine why each was a good president. Have each group share its information with the class by 1) role-playing a time-slip in which the presidents visit the class to describe their worlds; 2) introducing one of the group members dressed as the president in the proper time frame; 3) presenting a simulated television program that gives facts about each president; or 4) planning a birthday party for the presidents with appropriate presents for each man and reasons for the presents.

"Martin Luther King's Dream"

Ask students to tell what they know about the Nobel peace prize. Following a brainstorming session, have students research the date the first award was given, who the prize was given to and why, and the names of winners, particularly the person who won it in 1964. After students share what they learned about the Nobel peace prize, share pictures and information from *Meet Martin Luther King, Jr.* and *The Life and Death of Martin Luther King, Jr.* Ask students to discuss his ideas and dreams. Have them brainstorm ways we can help create a peaceful world and keep his dream of racial harmony and equality alive. After discussing the ideas, divide the class into groups to list five ways we can help at home and school to carry on the dream. Have each group make a paper-doll chain. On each doll, have a child write his or her name, birth date, and an action to promote world peace or racial equality. Display the paper dolls on a wall in the room with the words *We Celebrate a Dream* above the pictures.

"Thanksgiving Day"

Display *The Pilgrims of Plymouth*, *Molly's Pilgrim*, *Friendship's First Thanksgiving*, and *It's Thanksgiving* on the reading table with pictures of turkeys, corn, Pilgrims, and Native Americans. Have students, after looking at the pictures and books, write sentences stating what the pictures symbolize. Ask students to share their thoughts, and record any words or phrases associated with the first Thanksgiving. Add any words not suggested, such as Pilgrim, celebration, Native Americans, feast, and Mayflower. Discuss the words. Ask the students to listen as you read one of the books to determine whether the words listed on the board are mentioned in the book. Divide the class into collaborative groups to learn more about the first Thanksgiving. Have students find pictures and facts about the Pilgrims, the crops they grew, the role of the Indians in the Pilgrims' survival, and the weather at Plymouth settlement. After each group shares its findings, have students make two lists, one with reasons the Pilgrims were thankful that first year and the other with things we can be thankful for. Place a cornucopia in the center of a bulletin board with the heading *Reasons to Celebrate* above it. Have students copy reasons from their lists onto small cards and place the cards around the cornucopia.

Activities for Creative Arts

"Pop-Up Cards"

Place the book *How to Make Pop-Ups* on the art table with art supplies. Help students make pop-ups appropriate for the holiday being celebrated. Display the pop-ups on a display table or the bulletin board.

"Creative Drama"

After reading books related to a particular holiday, use creative drama to portray the first Thanksgiving, an Easter parade with hats made of construction paper and tissue paper, a St. Patrick's Day parade, the inauguration of a president, or a Maypole dance.

"Easter Eggs"

After reading *The Egg Tree*, have students design and make papier-mâché eggs, decorate hard-boiled eggs, or make eggs from construction paper or modeling dough. Hang the decorated eggs on an egg tree.

"Shadowboxes"

Shadowboxes for the various holidays can be made from construction paper, modeling clay, pipe cleaners, pictures, and other art supplies. These can be displayed with the books that students have read.

"Halloween"

After reading books about Halloween, have students make paper-plate masks for a bulletin-board display. Carve a pumpkin. Identify the stem and seeds, and plant the seeds for a science activity.

Bulletin Boards

"Our Nation Celebrates"

Have the students collect or draw holiday pictures to decorate a bulletin board entitled *Our Nation Celebrates*. Have students select a favorite holiday and write a few sentences about why the holiday is important. Hang the essays around the bulletin board.

"Thanksgiving—Then and Now"

In cooperative groups, have students create pictures representing the first Thanksgiving and a present-day Thanksgiving celebration. Place the heading Thanksgiving at the top center of the bulletin board. On the left side write Then; on the right write Now. Arrange the appropriate pictures beneath the headings.

Related Books

Easter

Houselander, Caryll. *Petook: An Easter Story*. Illustrated by Tomie dePaola. New York: Holiday House, 1988.
New life and the hope of spring's rebirth is illustrated by the birth of baby chicks.

Kraus, Robert. *How Spider Saved Easter*. Illustrated by the author. New York: Scholastic, 1988.
A spider spins his web into a beautiful Easter hat for his friend, Ladybug.

Milhouse, Katherine. *The Egg Tree*. Pictures by the author. New York: Charles Scribner's Sons, 1950. (Caldecott Award)
Katy and Carl have an Easter egg hunt, and their grandmother helps them make an egg tree.

Stevenson, James. *The Great Big Especially Beautiful Easter Egg*. New York: Greenwillow Books, 1983.
During his boyhood, Grandpa searches for an Easter egg to impress a young girl, and an unusual adventure results.

Supplemental Reading

Claret, Maria. *The Chocolate Rabbit*. Rev. by Jane O'Sullivan. Hauppauge, N.Y.: Barron's Educational Series, 1985.
A young rabbit accidentally helps to create a chocolate rabbit in this illustrated story.

Halloween

Ahlberg, Allan. *The Ghost Train*. Illustrated by André Amstutz. New York: Mulberry Books, 1992.
Three ghosts are scared by a ghost train.

Ahlberg, Janet, and Allan Ahlberg. *Funnybones*. New York: Mulberry Books, 1980.
The Skeleton family discovers they can have fun even when there is no one to scare.

Bunting, Eve. *Ghost's Hour, Spook's Hour*. Illustrated by Donald Carrick. Boston: Clarion Books, 1987.
A young boy who is lost in a creaky, dark house looks for the security of his mother.

Carlson, Natalie Savage. *Spooky and the Ghost Cat*. Illustrated by Andrew Glass. New York: Lothrop, Lee & Shepard, 1985.
Cats, spells, and broom rides spin a tale of Halloween.

Herman, Emily. *Hubknuckles*. Illustrated by Deborah Kogan Ray. New York: Crown, 1985.
A little girl is convinced that the ghost that dances every Halloween is her mother or father.

Prelutsky, Jack. *It's Halloween*. Illustrated by Marylin Hafner. New York: Greenwillow Books, 1977.
This book contains thirteen Halloween poems.

Williams, Linda. *The Little Old Lady Who Was Not Afraid of Anything*. Illustrated by Megan Lloyd. New York: Harper & Row (Harper Trophy Books), 1986.
This is a humorous story of an old lady who is chased through the woods by a spooky ghost who can disassemble himself.

Supplemental Reading

Ahlberg, Allan. *Skeleton Crew*. Illustrated by André Amstutz. New York: Mulberry Books, 1992.
Three vacationing ghosts encounter a pirate ship with a ghostly crew.

Gage, Wilson. *Mrs. Gaddy and the Ghost*. Illustrated by Marylin Hafner. New York: Mulberry Books, 1979.
Mrs. Gaddy attempts to get rid of a ghost.

Johnson, Tony. *The Vanishing Pumpkin*. Illustrated by Tomie dePaola. New York: G. P. Putnam's Sons, 1983.
Someone snitched a pumpkin from two very old witches.

Jewish Holidays

Hirsh, Marilyn. *I Love Passover*. Illustrated by the author. New York: Holiday House, 1985.
A young Jewish girl is taught the celebrations of her heritage.

Koralek, Jenny. *Hanukkah*. Illustrated by Juon Wijngaard. New York: Lothrop Lee & Shepard, 1990.
This version of the Hanukkah story features outstanding artwork.

Sussman, Susan. *There's No Such Thing as a Chanukah Bush, Sandy Goldstein*. Pictures by Charles Robinson. Niles, Ill.: Albert Whitman, 1983.
Sandy's grandfather teaches her that friend's can share their beliefs and celebrate together.

Supplemental Reading

Fisher, Aileen. *My First Hanukkah Book*. Illustrated by Priscila Kiedrowski. Chicago: Children's Press, 1985.
This book of poems explains many of the traditions of Hanukkah.

Kimmel, Eric. *Hershel and the Hanukkah Goblins*. Illustrated by Trina Schart Hyman. New York: Holiday House, 1985.
When Hershel discovers that the village people are not celebrating Hanukkah because of the goblins, he gets rid of the goblins.

Sussman, Susan. *Hanukkah: Eight Lights Around the World*. Illustrated by Judith Friedman. Chicago: Albert Whitman, 1988.
Eight short stories describe how young people in different countries celebrate the holiday.

Zalben, Jane Breskin. *Beni's First Chanukah*. Illustrated by the author. Salt Lake City: Henry Holt, 1988.
Beni enjoys his first celebration of family Chanukah traditions; a latke recipe is included.

Thanksgiving

Accorsi, William. *Friendship's First Thanksgiving*. Illustrated by the author. New York: Holiday House, 1992.
A dog named Friendship describes the colony's first year in the New World.

Cohen, Barbara. *Molly's Pilgrim*. Illustrated by Michael Deraney. New York: Lothrop Lee & Shepard, 1983.
A young immigrant teaches a class about pilgrims in this Thanksgiving story.

Cohen, Miriam. *Don't Eat Too Much Turkey*. Illustrated by Lillian Hoban. New York: Greenwillow Books, 1987.
A first-grade class gets ready for a Thanksgiving holiday.

Prelutsky, Jack. *It's Thanksgiving*. Illustrated by Marylin Hafner. New York: Greenwillow Books, 1982.
This book of poetry contains twelve Thanksgiving poems.

Sewell, Marcia. *The Pilgrims of Plymouth*. Illustrated by the author. New York: Atheneum, 1986.
A first-person narrative recounts the trials and accomplishments of the Pilgrims' first years.

Stevenson, James. *Fried Feathers for Thanksgiving*. New York: Greenwillow Books, 1986.
Emma, the witch, uses her skills in this entertaining story.

Valentine's Day

Carlson, Nancy. *Louanne Pig in the Mysterious Valentine*. Illustrated by the author. New York: Penguin (Puffin), 1987.
Louanne Pig tries to find who sent her the beautiful valentine.

Cohen, Miriam. *Bee My Valentine*. Illustrated by Lillian Hoban. New York: Greenwillow Books, 1978.
Jim solves the problem of George not getting many valentines.

Lexau, Joan. *Don't Be My Valentine*. Illustrated by Syd Hoff. New York: Harper & Row (I Can Read Books), 1983.
A nasty valentine falls into the teacher's hands.

Modell, Frank. *One Zillion Valentines*. Illustrated by the author. New York: Greenwillow Books, 1981.
Marvin and Milton decide to make valentines for everyone in the community.

Wittman, Sally. *The Boy Who Hated Valentine's Day*. Illustrated by Chaya Burstein. New York: Harper & Row, 1987.
When Ben forges his signature on his classmates' valentines, things take a turn for the worse.

Ziefert, Harriet, *Where Is Nicky's Valentine?* Illustrated by Richard Brown. New York: Penguin (Puffin), 1987.
With this lift-the-flap book, the reader searches for Nicky's valentine.

Other Holidays

Blassingame, Wyatt. *The Look-It-Up Book of Presidents*. New York: Random House, 1984.
The major accomplishments of presidents from Washington to Reagan are given.

De Kay, James. T. *Meet Martin Luther King, Jr*. New York: Random House, 1969.
This book about the life of Martin Luther King includes photographs.

Gross, Ruth Belov. *True Stories About Abraham Lincoln*. Illustrated by Jill Kastner. New York: Lothrop, Lee & Shepard, 1991.
A number of events in the life of Abraham Lincoln are covered.

Haskins, James. *The Life and Death of Martin Luther King, Jr.* New York: Lothrop, Lee & Shepard, 1977.
This book about the life of Martin Luther King is for children eight and older.

Irvine, Joan. *How to Make Pop-Ups.* Illustrated by Barbara Reid. New York: Beech Tree Books, 1987.
This book contains illustrations and directions for making pop-ups for a number of occasions.

Janice. *Little Bear Marches in the St. Patrick's Day Parade.* Illustrated by Mariana. New York: Lothrop, Lee & Shepard, 1967.
This book tells the adventure of a mouse and a bear in a parade.

Modell, Frank. *Look Out, It's April Fool's Day.* Illustrated by the author. New York: Greenwillow Books, 1985.
This story is a series of April Fools' Day tricks.

Schertle, Alice. *Jeremy Bean's St. Patrick's Day.* Illustrated by Linda Shute. New York: Lothrop, Lee & Shepard, 1987.
A school adventure about a boy not wearing green on St. Patrick's day.

Supplemental Reading

Kroll, Steven. *Happy Father's Day.* Illustrated by Marylin Hafner. New York: Holiday House, 1985.
This Father's Day story has special surprises for father.

———. *Happy Mother's Day.* Illustrated by Marylin Hafner. New York: Holiday House, 1985.
This book portrays the gifts for mother on her special day.

Author-Title Index

About the Authors

Barbara Beasley LeCroy is a former elementary teacher, children's librarian in a public library, and elementary school media specialist. She is currently the curriculum librarian for the College of Education and Psychology, director of the Gunn Education Materials Center, and an instructor in Curriculum and Instruction at the University of Southern Mississippi. She conducts workshops in storytelling, and has been a member of the National Council of Teachers of English Storytelling Committee for the past eight years. She is a specialist in storytelling, curriculum, and children's literature, and has made numerous national, regional, and state presentations.

Bonnie Hensley Holder is a former elementary teacher, junior high school reading teacher, and Mississippi State Department of Education Consultant. She recently retired from the Department of Curriculum and Instruction at the University of Southern Mississippi where she served as Coordinator of Undergraduate Programs. While at the university, she published articles, made presentations at the state, regional, and national conventions, and conducted in-service sessions for area schools on issues related to reading methods and children's literature. She has served as recording secretary for the Mississippi Reading Association and is currently on the Board of Directors.